TEACH YOURSELF

DRIED FLOWERS

Judith Blacklock

Hodder & Stoughton

A MEMBER OF THE HODDER HEADLINE GROUP

British Library Cataloguing in Publication Data

Blacklock, Judith
  Dried Flowers. – (Teach Yourself Series)
  I. Title II. Series
  745.92

ISBN 0-340-59432-2

First published 1993
Impression number 10 9 8 7 6 5 4 3 2 1
Year   1998 1997 1996 1995 1994 1993

Typeset by Rowland Phototypesetting Ltd, Bury St Edmunds, Suffolk
Printed in Great Britain for Hodder & Stoughton Educational,
a division of Hodder Headline PLC, Mill Road, Dunton Green,
Sevenoaks, Kent by Cox and Wyman Ltd, Reading, Berks.

—————— CONTENTS ——————

Acknowledgements

All designs are by the author, except for: Figure 24, Jennifer Hardyment; Figure 25, Lilian Tyson; Figure 26, Doreen Fox; Figure 33, Frances Beal; Figure 35, Mary Gwyther; Figure 36, Betty Gravestock.

The author would like to thank David Blacklock and Alice ter Haar for their help and advice and Adrian Whiteley at RHS Wisley for his knowledge on nomenclature.

The author and the publishers would like to thank the following for generously supplying material of such high quality:

Dried flowers

Robson Watley International
2a Pembroke Road, Bromley, Kent BR1 2RU. Tel: 081 466 0830.

Silk flowers

H Andreas Ltd
Unit 10, Hortonwood 32, Telford, Shropshire TF1 4EX.
Tel: 0952 670399.

Parchment flowers

Ascalon Design
The Coach House, Aylesmore Court, St Briavels, Glos GL15 6UQ.
Tel: 0594 530567.

Candles

Candle Makers Supplies
28 Blythe Road, London W14 0HA. Tel: 071 602 4031.
Shop and mail order.

Photographs by Roddy Paine

Illustrations by Kate Simunek

—— INTRODUCTION ——

Arranging flowers which can be displayed for a considerable time is extremely satisfying. It gives full vent to your creative abilities and is wonderfully relaxing. You can lose yourself in it for hours. The techniques are straightforward and easy to learn. Although some of the design principles are the same as for fresh flowers, there is much that is only applicable to the selection and design of dried and silk arrangements. Essentially you are creating a long-lasting piece that will be part of the decoration of your home in the same way as your fabrics, wallpaper and furniture.

Long-lasting flowers do not need to be expensive. There is a wealth of material that is free if you use your eyes, and much that is inexpensive if you know what to do and what to look for. With this book you will be able to create a host of delightful designs that need not cost a fortune and will enhance your home all year round.

Over the centuries many cultures have dried flowers for use in medicines, potions, fragrances and dyes, and in many other ways that improved the quality of life. Their function was either symbolic or practical until the eighteenth century when it became fashionable to display dried flowers purely for decoration.

Times change, but preserved plant material continues to play an important role in many facets of life. Many of the ingredients of modern medicines are plant based. Fragrances are still made from flower petals. Plants are still used for natural dyes. Dried herbs add flavour to cooking. Flower arrangements add colour, fragrance and beauty to our homes. Rare indeed is the home without dried flowers. Old fashioned flowers may spill out of a basket in the bedroom. There may be a rose-studded topiary tree in the dining-room, a dried herb wreath in the kitchen. There

— 1 —

may even be a dusty half-forgotten gift of long-faded blooms high on a shelf and needing help.

Dried flowers will never lose their charm, and one hopes the day will never come when they cease to be used to beautify the home. Over the past few years, however, exciting new artificial plant material has been introduced of such high quality that can, if used correctly, only enhance the natural beauty of dried flowers. Long gone are the days when any artificial stem was considered the very worst of taste, akin to the plastic daffodils and roses given away free with a box of washing powder. Today, artificial flowers made from silk, polyester or parchment, and artificial fruits, are so realistic that they can fool even the keenest of eyes. They do not have a natural fragrance but keep their colour and can be of special interest to those who suffer from hay fever and dust allergies.

Interest in long-lasting arrangements has also developed through a different style of arranging now practised in this country. This style, which first became popular in Europe, is very easy to copy and has been termed 'modern style' in this book. Although there is a great deal of interest in this modern style, for many, the traditional arrangements remain a source of great satisfaction.

But if all plant material, dried and artificial, has its own beauty why do you need this book? It advises you on how to select your flowers from the wealth of material that is available, so that you will get maximum value for your money. It shows you how to invest your money wisely through selection of freshly dried material with good colour and strong stems. Advice is given on how these mediums can be mixed together to take best advantage of all the different features, resulting in innovative designs with exciting colouring that will dispel the dead flower myth forever.

You will learn the need for contrast of shape and texture to give impact to the design. This book provides information on growing plant material for drying, but, in order not to confuse, only those plants which are particularly useful and can easily be purchased if preferred are included. Perhaps most importantly, this book gives you the technical knowledge that will enable you not only to copy all the ideas found in this book and any other ideas that you may see at home or abroad in restaurants, shops or hotels, but will also give you the confidence to go out and create something entirely new that comes from your own individual flair and imagination. This book will open the doors to your own personal creativity, and enable you to give your home distinctive style, with an atmosphere of warmth and welcome.

1

—— HOW TO START ——

Over the last few years there have been many changes in the world of dried flower arranging or flower design as it is often now called. In part this has been due to the increase in the varieties of dried flowers that are available, many of which are now grown commercially in this country to a very high standard. Dried flowers are currently being used to create innovative and exciting new designs and styles through the interchange of ideas with those living on the Continent. There are now wonderful artificial flowers available, made from parchment, polyester and 'silk'. Plastic fruits and seedheads can be so realistic that it is hard to distinguish them from the real thing. Although these are not natural plant material and lack a natural fragrance they do have stems that can be angled at will and do not break. They can give an intensity of colour that does not readily fade and they are easy to care for.

With the profusion of material available to make the home more attractive it can be difficult to know where to start. If you have an understanding of the basic elements of design as well as a good grasp of the techniques required to hold the materials in place, you will be able to realise virtually all the designs that you have admired in shops and magazines.

Flower arranging is also a creative art and if you understand why an arrangement looks good, you will be able to not only copy but also to design. This chapter will help you to understand and design both traditional and modern arrangements.

Traditional, modern and _____ modern-traditional designs

To understand the differences between these styles first look at the following photographs in the colour sections. Figure 8 shows a traditional design, Figures 6 and 7 show modern designs and Figure 9 shows a modern-traditional design.

Traditional design

These are designs that have been popular for centuries. The main features are:

- Stems radiating from a central *point.*
- A wide variety of plant material harmoniously woven through the design.
- Often some space within the design to show off the beauty of the individual plant material.

Modern design

Over the past few years a style of dried flower arranging has developed in this country based on the dried flower work of the continental florists. Both vertical and groundwork designs fall into this category.

The main features are:

- Each stem has its own point of origin.
- Each variety of plant material is blocked together to give lines or areas of colour, form and texture.
- Each variety of plant material frequently rises to a uniform height.
- There is usually a base covering, or groundwork, of flowers, seed-heads, moss, etc. from which taller stems may arise. A design feature is often made of these bare stems.

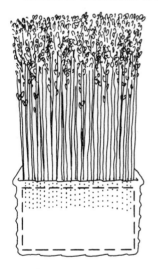 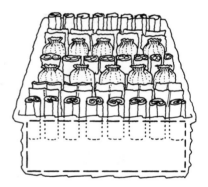

Modern-traditional design

This style takes features from both of the above categories. It can be summed up by:

- All the stems appear to radiate from a central *area*.
- Each variety of plant material is blocked to give an area of colour, form and texture.
- There is little or no space within the design.

These styles, with examples, are fully explained in chapters 7, 8 and 9.

Dried flower arranging can be incredibly messy so prepare well before you start. Put a cloth or sheet on the table on which you are working, and another on the floor underneath the working area.

2

— DESIGN ELEMENTS —

Even though you can envisage the style you wish to create it can be difficult to know where to start with the profusion of plant material on display in shops, garden centres and speciality shops – even if you could afford to buy a bunch of every variety. Whether you prefer to grow and dry your own plant material or buy all your needs directly from a shop, you need to select plant material with an awareness of form, colour, texture and space.

Form

Form is the term for a three-dimensional object as opposed to shape which refers to the two dimensions, i.e. something that is flat. As plant material is three-dimensional the word *form* is used in this book.

All plant material whether natural or artificial, can be divided into one of three forms – branching, line and focal, full descriptions of which follow. These materials are used in the majority of traditional designs. There is a predominance of line and focal material in modern designs and in the modern-traditional style, focal and branching material is mainly used.

Branching plant material

Branching material has interest not just at the tip of a stem like a daisy but continuing down the stem on branches off the main stem. Each branch bears flowers or seedheads. Examples are sea lavender, marjoram, oats, barley, gypsophila and many types of foliage.

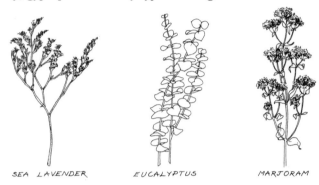

SEA LAVENDER   EUCALYPTUS   MARJORAM

Branching plant material is less emphatic than line material. The colours are generally soft and understated. Because it is multi-headed and multi-branched, often with gentle curves, the overall effect is natural and flowing. The dried stems can be angled to flow over the sides of the container so that it becomes part of the overall design. By virtue of these characteristics branching material is used

- in traditional arrangements:
  - to create a soft outline or shape;
  - to fill out the design and help hide the bare stems of the other more rigid plant material; and
  - to give a relaxed gentle overall feel, reminiscent of an English country garden.
- in modern-traditional, and in some modern arrangements, tightly bunched together to give an area of colour, form and texture.

Line plant material

This category of plant material looks as it sounds. Line material has interest – be it flowers, seedheads or foliage – not only at the tip of the single stem but also clustered closely down and around the stem, forming more or less a line. Examples are lavender, larkspur and amaranthus.

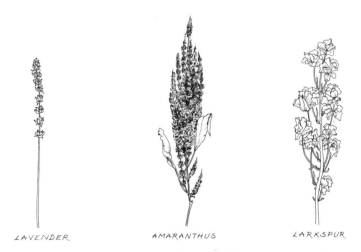

LAVENDER   *AMARANTHUS*   *LARKSPUR*

Such stems tend to be rather straight and rigid. Because of its rigidity line material is not used as much in traditional arrangements as branching and focal material but is used a great deal in modern designs.

Line material is used

- in traditional work:
  — to reinforce the shape created by the branching material;
  — to act as a transitional shape between branching and focal material; and
  — to help hide the bare stems of the other material.
- in modern work where the uniformity given by a regimented row of parallel stems creates a block of colour, form and texture.
- in modern-traditional work where it is bunched to give blocked interest of colour, form and texture and perhaps fragrance.

Focal material

This refers to plant material where the interest is focused at the tip of the stem. The stem itself is usually bare. This is because the leaves of flowers become very brittle when dried by the most common methods, making them impractical to use even if they remain on the stem. The shape of the flower head is usually roundish. Examples are helichrysums, roses, peonies and hydrangeas.

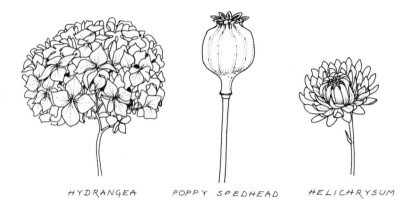

HYDRANGEA   POPPY SPEDHEAD   HELICHRYSUM

Focal material is used to give emphasis and focal interest. It is essential in most dried flower designs to:

- give strength to the design, for round shapes have a strong visual pull;
- give interest through contrast of form.

Chapter 4 gives details of plant material useful to the flower arranger and states whether it is branching, focal or line.

Texture

The selection and judicious placing of material with contrasting textures is a key factor for successful flower design. If texture is not carefully considered your resulting arrangements will, in all probability, be fussy and uninteresting.

Texture is the way you imagine an object will feel to the touch – a teasel prickly, a pebble smooth, bark rough. A good example of contrasting texture can be seen in a mushroom. The top is smooth, yet turn it upside down and the texture appears deceptively rough. To enhance the qualities of texture, contrast is essential. Try placing a teasel and a fir cone either side of an upside-down mushroom or fungus. See how fussy and busy they appear when positioned next to each other. Turn the mushroom or fungus the other way up to show its smooth upper surface and the appearance of the teasel and pine cone is immediately enhanced.

PINE CONE   MUSHROOM   TEAZLE

PINE CONE   MUSHROOM   TEAZLE

The majority of plant material dried by the hanging method – which is probably the simplest method of preserving plant material – undergoes a change in petal shape when dried. Once the moisture is removed the petals shrink and curl. The general textural appearance of much dried material is therefore intricate or rough rather than smooth. The same is true of polyester and silk flowers which have been produced to imitate dried rather than fresh flowers. For this type of texture to be shown off to best advantage try to include one type of plant material in every design with a plainer, smoother texture. Examples of a plainer texture can be seen in poppy seedheads, Chinese lanterns, honesty seedpods, cinnamon sticks, golden mushrooms, and many artificial fruits and glycerined foliage (details on how to glycerine are in Appendix 2). Dried flower producers are now marketing a range of glycerined foliage which has been dyed to give the appearance of fresh foliage. Eucalyptus is perhaps the most widely available foliage of this kind. Eucalyptus can be hang-dried and still retain a smooth texture.

Colour

Perhaps the most exciting part of flower arranging is choosing the colours you wish to put together. Thankfully, long-lasting flower arrangements have lost their image of dead flowers collecting dust. Not only can you mix artificial flowers with dried to give more vibrant colour, but the use of dyes has also led to a greater colour range of dried flowers themselves.

Colour is to a large extent a question of taste. Careful drying of flowers means their colours can now be clear and interesting rather than sad and faded. Do remember that whatever colours you choose, your dried plant material will fade with time. The fading process will accelerate if the materials are:

- exposed to strong sunlight; or
- placed in a smoky atmosphere.

If you wish your design to remain as attractive as when newly completed you will need to replace some of your plant material at regular intervals. Some dried flowers will need to be replaced every year as they fade and get dusty. There are several aerosol products now on sale which contain a cleaner to dissolve dust particles and a propellant to blow them gently away. Two trade names are Fisons Flower Cleaner and Petal Fresh. These products are available from many garden centres and mail order companies. Try adding 'silk' or parchment flowers to your dried flower arrangement. They add interest and retain their colour longer.

Before buying any materials you should first consider where you are going to place the completed design. Look at the furnishings in the room and pick out two or three of the colours that complement each other.

The colour wheel

Red, yellow and blue are primary colours. They are the basic colours from which others are made and constitute the large main petals on the flower colour wheel shown below. These colours are pure and strong and are more likely to be seen in fast-food restaurants and in children's toy shops rather than in dried flower shops. If different combinations of these colours are mixed together in equal amounts they produce the secondary colours, green, yellow and orange. These are shown as the secondary petals of the flower colour wheel below. If these six colours are mixed with the colours closest to them they produce six more colours: yellow-orange, yellow-green, blue-green, blue-violet, red-violet and red-orange.

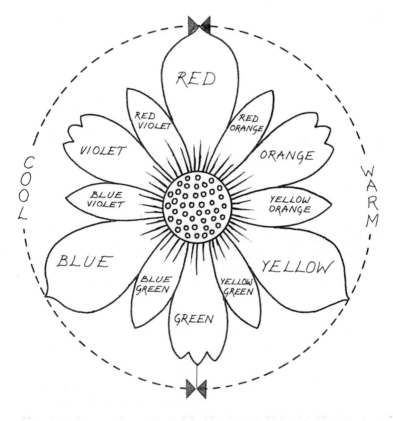

These 12 strong pure colours have powerful personalities and are usually used only to give accent in dried flower designs. Some dried flowers such as physalis, marigolds, sunflowers and some helichrysums and statice do have these characteristics, along with many dyed flowers and seedheads. Generally, however, dried flowers have softer, more muted colours which have been created by the addition of varying amounts of white, grey or black to the pure colour. The colour variations created by these additions go on for ever. If white is added to one of the colours on the wheel, a tint is created, such as light blue (light blue statice). The addition of grey creates a tone such as grey blue (globe thistle) and a black shade, such as dark blue (many varieties of lavender).

Green is nature's colour, reflecting the light rays of the sun in their most soothing form. With flowers green never overpowers but acts as a harmonizer to bring other colours together. Consequently, green is the ideal background for all traditional dried flower work. Its importance is also recognised in modern work where the green of stems or a cushion of moss brings the design back to a natural form.

Start with green as your background colour and then go on to choose your colour scheme. Many people think in terms of a peach colour scheme or a pink colour scheme. If your choice is pink, think of two, three or four colours in the same section of the wheel and use a mixture of their tints, tones and shades, rather than thinking of pure colours. If you do this you cannot go wrong. You could, for example, choose pink roses (a tint of red), lavender (a shade of blue-violet), marjoram (a shade of violet), with a touch of pure blue (larkspur) to give accent.

If, on the other hand, you choose peach, you could create a design with peach roses (a tint of orange), goldenrod (a shade of yellow-orange), *Achillea millefolium* (a tint of yellow) and *Alchemilla mollis* (a tint of yellow-green). The accent flowers could be marigolds (pure yellow or orange) or Chinese lanterns (orange). Dark brown glycerined beech or oak would give added depth and interest to this colour scheme.

If you are unsure about colour start by limiting the number of colours that you use and allow one to dominate to avoid conflict.

Warm and cool colours

The hues from red to yellow, including pink, brown and burgundy, are warm colours, and those from green to violet, including blue, and all the shades of grey, are cool colours. Yellow when introduced to a cool colour scheme becomes cool. Green, as always, is the harmoniser. Warm colours are cheerful and demand attention whereas cool colours are generally calm and more subdued.

If you mix warm and cool colours it is the warm colours that will dominate. Add shades, rather than tints, of cool colours into a warm colour scheme, i.e. those which have been darkened with the addition of black, for example, midnight blue, deep red. Conversely, if you wish to introduce warm colours into a cool background choose those which are tints rather than shades, i.e. those which have been lightened with the addition of white, for example, cream and apricot.

These are guidelines to give you the confidence to choose original colour schemes.

The seasons

You may wish to relate the colours of your arrangement according to the season. In the garden blue is in evidence from January through to late autumn. Yellow, green and white are always refreshing at Easter time. In summer there is a riotous profusion of all colours available. In autumn one tends to think of burgundy, bronze, gold and orange. The traditional Christmas colours are, of course, red and green.

If you prefer a light pastel effect do remember that a little of a darker colour, such as a deep shade of green, will highlight your flowers without subduing the overall effect. Conversely, if you are using dark autumnal colours lift the design with the addition of, perhaps, peach. If you are using shades of red and green at Christmas give them a lift with the addition of a little yellow, bright gold or scarlet berries or flowers.

Individual colours

The additional information below on individual colours may also help.

Green

For any work with flowers, fresh, dried, silk or parchment, green is the harmoniser. Traditional arrangements in particular rely on the incorporation of the colour green. When working with fresh flowers green is readily available – it is more difficult when working with dried, silk and parchment flowers but green is still available. Examples of dried green plant material are oats, barley, grasses and linseed but it is very important that you buy fresh stock which is still green and has not turned to an oatmeal colour. Naturally green plant material tends to fade quite quickly. If you leave grasses long enough they actually turn to hay. Do replace them unless you want the feel of an autumnal display. Lightly pressed foliage, such as sprays of bracken, fern or green beech, is suitable, as is glycerined foliage to which a few drops of green dye have been added.

A certain amount of commercially dyed plant material is extremely realistic and should be considered, but do avoid the more lurid colours. If you use only one variety and one colour of dyed plant material in an otherwise natural arrangement you will confuse all but the experts. Commercially produced dyed material is either dyed externally, when treated plant material is dipped in vats of dye, or internally, when the fresh plant material drinks a solution of glycerine, water and dye. The latter method is extremely realistic. It is expensive but often worth it. Preserved eucalyptus is attractive, easy to use, and is often available in shops. Silk foliage is now sold in many department stores and garden centres along with silk and parchment flowers, and if this is carefully mixed with dried flowers few will be any the wiser.

Green is the ideal colour to create the framework of your traditional designs. If the outline of a design is created with a strong colour it will overpower the other plant material. The eye quickly tires of strong colour and the design may well look top heavy. If you wish to use a lot of different colours in your design they will always look good if you also include a good deal of green.

Yellow

Yellow is a cheerful colour which gives a sense of well-being. It can be mixed with cool or warm colours and takes on their nature. A clear yellow is wonderful for adding bright, fresh, vibrant colour to an arrangement, especially in a design composed mainly of darker colours. Examples are yellow statice and *Achillea millefolium*. Yellow-orange, as seen in sunflowers and *Achillea filipendulina*, lies in the warm half of the colour wheel and is consequently happy mixed with orange, peach and rust colours.

Orange

Orange-coloured plant material can be difficult. It can be so vibrant, as seen in carthamus with the orange centre, Chinese lanterns and orange marigolds, that it is happiest mixed with other oranges, browns, peaches and yellows that are close on the colour wheel. Blue is directly opposite orange on the colour wheel and if they are combined the result is a very vibrant colour scheme.

Peach is very popular in dried flower arranging but there are few flowers that dry naturally in this tint. Do consider commercially dyed plant material that has been treated carefully and subtly. Peach is evident in many artificial flowers (perhaps even more than nature intended!). Many grasses and, for example, *Achillea filipendulina*, are often dyed successfully. Peach tints do lift and give liveliness to long-lasting flower arrangements and harmonise with the decor in many homes.

Red

Dark red flowers such as roses and amaranthus give depth of colour and strength to an arrangement. Light red flowers can light up a design and give it vitality.

Pink lifts and gives life to an arrangement. It is lovely used with deeper pinks, blues, greens and greys. Pink flowers that dry well are larkspur, roses, helichrysums, peonies and statice.

Violet and purple

Most violet and purple flowers dry to a soft mellow colour which is easy to add to almost any design successfully. Examples are marjoram and purple statice. Liatris has a vibrant violet colour.

Blue

It is rare to see a Dutch flower painting that does not have a touch of blue. The Dutch artists always considered blue to bring life to the other colours in a painting. So it is with dried flower designs. The strong vibrant blues as seen in cornflowers and larkspur enhance many designs, particularly those made up of pinks and greens. Softer blues seen in lavender and mintflower are mellow and can be used with any colour combination.

Brown

The colour brown is a mixture of the three primary colours – red, blue and yellow. Many of the new exciting plant materials imported from Africa, India and South America are in tints, tones and shades of brown, as are many seedheads, cones and nuts found in this country. So too is most glycerined foliage. Many grasses and cereals turn an oatmeal colour if they have been picked too late in the season or if they are old stock. If an arrangement consists of predominantly brown plant material it tends to have an autumnal feel. If this is the case and you wish your arrangement to be on display all year round, try adding plant material with a lively colour to the display, for example, white larkspur, lemon statice or pale pink helichrysums. Dark brown plant material looks particularly attractive mixed with yellows and oranges (see Figure 15, colour section).

White/cream

White and soft cream coloured flowers lift the colours they are mixed with. The eye is strongly attracted to the colour white and therefore it must be used judiciously. If you use white with dark colours you might find that at a distance the white stands our too starkly. If your container is white it is advisable to use some white flowers in the design to provide a link between plant material and container. Larkspur, *Achillea millefolium* 'The Pearl', helichrysum, statice and sea lavender are examples of white/cream dried plant material.

Containers and colour

One way of choosing a colour combination is to use your container as inspiration. If your container is metal the following colours would be suitable.

- Greys, pinks and blues for pewter.
- Yellows and peaches for brass.
- Peaches, apricots and creams for copper.
- Pinks, blues and whites for silver.

There is no need to use these colours exclusively but blue lavender in pewter, yellow achillea in brass and apricot helichrysums in a copper container will form a link and bring out the individual quality of the metal used. Orange and burgundy colours in pewter look unhappy. Pink colours are enhanced by copper and silver rather than brass.

If your container is a dark colour and you are using predominantly dark material, try lifting the design by adding pastel tints. Conversely, if your container is a light colour, say bleached basketry, try including some dark material to give depth and to highlight the pastel tints.

Space

In traditional designs space is used within the flower arrangement to show off the individual form, colour and texture of each individual stem of flowers or seedheads. Stems are placed at various angles so that all the different aspects of the flowering stem can be seen and appreciated. As all stems appear to radiate from a central point there is obviously more space at the outside of the design rather than at the centre.

In modern design space is sometimes at the centre of the design. In a groundwork design there is no space within the arrangement.

In modern-traditional design the blocking of plant material means that there will be virtually no space within the design.

Whichever style of design you create you should position it in an open area. Do not place it on a narrow shelf so that it looks squashed in, or on the top of a kitchen unit where it scrapes the ceiling. Any arrangement need to be surrounded by space in order to be fully appreciated.

Once you gain confidence and begin to experiment you will find with your new found skills that many of these 'rules' can successfully be broken. Good use of form, texture, colour and space is essential in good dried flower design but the principles of design – balance, scale, contrast, rhythm, proportion, dominance and harmony – are also important and these are discussed in the next chapter.

3

– DESIGN PRINCIPLES –

Balance, scale, contrast, rhythm, dominance, proportion and harmony might sound tremendously complicated but the theory behind these principles of design is easily understood. Understanding them will help you to design creative arrangements easily.

Balance

Good balance means that not only will your design not fall over, but it will also not *look* as if it might. Good balance is important whatever style you wish to create.

Good balance is helped by good proportion. Other facts that will help you to achieve good balance are:

- Containers with two handles, or one central handle, will simplify the balance. If you have a container with asymmetrical balance, such as a jug, the single handle should form part of the overall design (look at Figure 28, colour section).
- Keep stronger focal material within the limits created by the branching outline material otherwise the design can become top heavy.
- Use lighter colours at the limits of your design and stronger or brighter colours lower and more central in traditional designs. The purer the colour the more eye-catching it is. The eye feels more comfortable with strong coloured material within the design rather than on the boundaries.

*material
angled over rim
of container*

- In traditional and modern-traditional designs angle some plant material down over the rim of your container. This will give the plant material and the container the appearance of belonging to each other, otherwise the plant material can appear to be uncomfortably perched on its container.
- For many designs a base can be an aid to good balance. If the width of plant material in a completed design is greater than one and a half times the width of the container, at its widest point, it can make your design appear top heavy. The addition of a simple base, repeating the approximate shape of your overall design – that is to say a round base for a round arrangement or an oval base for an oval arrangement, can give extra width at the base, thus correcting the balance. A base can be almost anything flat, for example, a tray, a table mat, a covered cake board, a silver tray or a bread board (see Figure 28 in the colour section). Baskets tend to look awkward placed on a base. They need to have direct contact with the furniture or ledge on which they are placed.

Scale

If all the parts that make up your design look as if they belong to the same family then your use of scale is correct. This means that:

- Your container should be the right size for the plant material you will use – large flowers and seedpods, such as Chinese lanterns and hydrangeas, need a container such as a heavy pottery jug or a large basket whereas delicate spray roses and gypsophila would be in scale with a small glass bowl or a china dish.

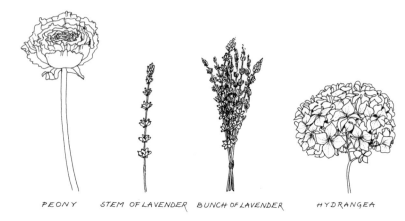

PEONY   STEM OF LAVENDER   BUNCH OF LAVENDER   HYDRANGEA

- Your flowers should be in scale with each other – peonies and hydrangeas are not in scale with a single stem of lavender. If, however, ten or eleven stems of lavender are bunched together and wired or taped as one the effect would be bolder and therefore would be more in scale.
- No one type of flower should be more than twice the size of the next largest in the arrangement. If it is add some transitional material of an in-between size.

If your focal flowers appear too large to be in scale with the other plant material, and they are the only flower of that colour in the arrangement, add line or branching material of the same colour and the focal flowers will appear less dominant.

Contrast

Contrast of shape is important in most designs but contrast of texture is always a priority. It enhances all designs where more than one variety of plant material is used. Where one type of flower or seedhead is tightly massed, contrast can be achieved through the use of a container with a different texture or perhaps making a feature out of smooth bare stems.

Rhythm

Rhythmic designs are those that hold the viewer's attention. Attention is held because there is movement within the design. Rhythm is created by placing plant material so that the eye moves round the arrangement, lingering on it rather than moving away. So how can you obtain rhythm in your design?

Traditional designs

- Radiate stems from a central *point*. In traditional designs all stems appear to originate from one point – this builds up rhythm through repetition of movement from this central position.
- Place strong shapes central to the design (focal material) and finer plant material at the outer limits (branching material), linking them with line material so that the eye moves smoothly from one shape to the next.
- Weave plant material through the design. For this reason it is better to avoid too many varieties of plant material in a small design unless they are strongly linked by colour.

Modern designs

- Repetition of parallel stems.
- Where more than one variety of plant material is used the juxtapositioning of colour, form and texture.

Modern-traditional designs

- Radiate the stems from a central *area*.
- Repetition of different colours, forms and textures in the grouping of plant material.

Proportion

The rules of good proportion were established by the ancient Greeks. The theory is that unequal distribution of visual weight is more pleasing to the human eye than equal distribution. Ideal proportion exists when two parts of a whole are divided in the ratio 3:2. If ratios seem complicated think in terms of thirds – one part will be two thirds of the second part.

Traditional designs

As a guideline:

- (a) the volume of your flowers should be approximately one and a half times the volume of your container, or

- (b) the height of the plant material should be approximately one and a half times the height of the container, or one and a half times the width, whichever is the greater.
- (c) the width of the plant material should be about one and a half times the width of the container at its widest point. Any more and the design may appear unbalanced.

It is as simple as that.

If you find you have overpowered your container with an exuberance of plant material you can adjust this by adding a base under the container. If this harmonises well you will find you have created better proportion and better balance by this quick and easy means.

the addition of a base can give better proportion

If your container is deep-based and has a low handle, for example, a basket, do not smother the handle. Good proportion can be achieved by allowing lots of plant material to be angled so that it comes right down the sides of the basket, or by letting the basket dominate the plant material, in the ratio 3:2. If you want a traditional design choose a basket with modest sides and good space between the rim and the handle.

Modern designs

Good modern designs can sometimes seem to break the rule of good proportion. For example, when the height is exaggerated to give strong upward movement, a closer look will show that even if the container is disproportionately small to the plant material, or vice versa, the rule of 3:2 remains true in the placing of plant material within the design and in the volume used. In the modern design in Figure 18 (colour section) the amount of lavender to roses is in the approximate proportion 3:2.

Modern-traditional designs

The volume of plant material to the container is usually in the ratio 3:2.

Dominance

Rivalry is created when two parts of a whole, for example, container and plant material, have equal importance. Both parts vie with each other to capture your attention.

Traditional arrangements

Plant material should be more dominant than the container.

Modern arrangements

Depending on the type of modern design the plant material or the container will be more dominant.

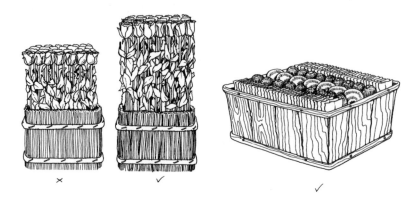

Modern-traditional arrangements

The plant material is usually more dominant. Although the plant material is not tall it creates a strong mass of colour, form and texture which is visually dominant.

For any style you should use colour carefully. Avoid equal amounts of two strong colours, for example, pure yellow and shocking pink, as they will fight with each other for dominance – rather like two strong characters in a partnership. Use more of one than the other. With more subdued, less attention-seeking colours, the problem is not as acute, but one colour in an arrangement should always dominate.

Harmony

If you succeed in using the above principles of design you will have harmony in your arrangement and good harmony means that your flowers have the same feel. Silk orchids can look out of place in a basket of cereals and herbs. Your arrangement should also suit the room in which it is positioned. A selection of grasses look great in the kitchen but might look out of place in a formal drawing room where roses and eucalyptus would be more in keeping with the decor.

4

DRIED PLANT MATERIAL

There is nothing more daunting to the novice flower arranger than to be faced with an endless choice of dried flowers, whether in a garden centre, department store, specialist shop, or at the florists. This chapter gives guidance on how to choose a combination of dried plant material that will make a cohesive design, and how to select quality flowers. Details on how to dry flowers and seedheads at home are given in Appendix 1. It is an uncomplicated and very satisfying hobby.

Dried flower designing requires more plant material than many beginners would believe possible, far more than for fresh flower work. Do not be perturbed, however, as it does not have to be expensive. The different plant materials mentioned in this chapter are readily available throughout the world. All can be purchased or grown from seed on a small piece of land, on a patio or even in a window box. Although the plant materials listed all have good reasons for being included in this chapter it is certainly not necessary to assemble them all. Start with those that you find easy to acquire or grow. Many varieties of wild plant material are excellent, but as they are rarely found in shops they have only been included in Appendix 6 where you will also find information on other plant material.

Each of the varieties of plant material has been divided into sections headed branching, line or focal. Where a variety can fall into more than one category this is mentioned. Varieties that have a smooth section have the symbol 'S'. This information will help you to get started and to develop confidence so that you can create your own designs.

In each case, the botanical name is given followed by the commonly-used name. Elsewhere in the book, each variety of plant material is referred to only by its common name. In some parts of the country the plant material may also be known by another common name.

If you are interested in traditional and modern-traditional designs you will need, as a rough guide, about five different varieties of dried flowers and seedheads. For modern work you may only need one, such as lavender.

For traditional designs you should try to use at least one example each of branching, line and focal material. For modern designs line and focal forms are mainly used, and for modern-traditional styles focal and branching plant material have great importance. For any style you should try and include at least one variety with a smooth texture.

Any unused flowers should be stored carefully in a dark dry place so that you can build up a stock of a wide range of materials. Alternatively they can be hung upside-down to become an attractive room feature, but the colour will fade more rapidly. The vast majority of flowers and seedheads used in the colour sections are mentioned in this chapter.

—— Branching plant material ——

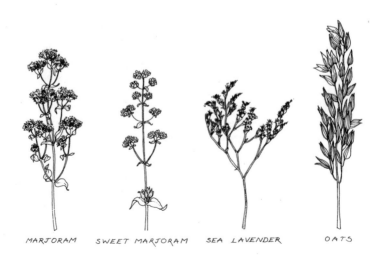

MARJORAM   SWEET MARJORAM   SEA LAVENDER   OATS

Figure 1 Parchment tulips and dried aspidistra leaves with the bare stems of corkscrew willow

Figure 2 Floral ring (see page 109)

Figure 3 Modern-traditional design

Figure 4 Parchment auriculas, artificial fruits and 'silk' pansies with glycerined bear grass

Figure 5 Decorated basket

Figure 6 Modern groundwork design

Figure 7 Modern vertical design

Figure 8 Traditional design

Figure 9 Modern-traditional design

Figure 10 Traditional design of dried hydrangeas, peonies, poppy seedheads 'Hen and Chickens', globe thistles, eucalyptus, larkspur and peach anaphalis

Figure 11 Shells, larkspur, sea lavender, lagarus and roses

Figure 12 Eucalyptus, achillea, broom bloom, helichrysums and peonies

Origanum vulgare (Marjoram)

Marjoram is the most delightful herb that can be included in just about any design. Unlike many herbs, such as rosemary and thyme, which are very brittle, marjoram has a sturdy stem. It has glorious purple-blue flowers, is fragrant, and gives softness, yet body, to any design. It is easy to grow and not expensive if purchased from the dried flower shop. What more can one ask?

To grow or to purchase fresh

Marjoram is an easy-growing hardy perennial, which is so pretty it will enhance any flower garden. The flowers should be picked for drying immediately after flowering. Fresh marjoram can sometimes be obtained from pick-your-own farms, or can be found in some florists shops.

To purchase dried

The length of stem can vary. Some bunches are very much shorter than others so if you wish to use marjoram in a large flowering design watch for the length of stem. Similarly, some bunches are more densely covered with the purple blue flowers than others, and the colour more intense, so make your selection carefully.

Origanum marjorana (S)
(Sweet marjoram)

Sweet marjoram is another robust fragrant herb. It has a soft grey-green colour and looks very effective when combined with pink and blue flowers.

To grow or to purchase fresh

Sweet marjoram is easily grown as a hardy annual. The stems should be cut just before the flowers open, and should be as long as possible.

To purchase dried

As with marjoram, the stem lengths of sweet marjoram can vary considerably, so consider your arrangement before purchasing.

Limonium dumosum, syn. Statice tatarica (Sea lavender)

Sea lavender seems to have been around for a very long time. It is so often used unimaginatively that it might be difficult to accept it as a useful addition to the dried flower collection. However, it can be used to great effect because:

- it covers dried foam cheaply and effectively;
- it is generally available throughout the country; and
- it is available in a wide variety of colours although the natural fresh white or the dyed green are most useful.

Sea lavender grows on stems that have a natural curve. When placing it in a container use the stems to advantage by ensuring that the arch of the stem curves 'downwards' away from the central axis and over the rim of your container.

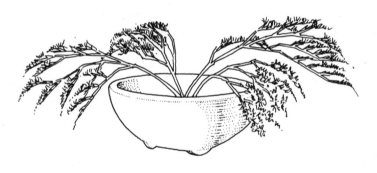

SEA LAVENDER

To grow or to purchase fresh

Sea lavender is a perennial and will take two years to produce a flower, so perhaps for the eager flower arranger it would be better to buy plants from the garden centre. However, for those prepared to wait, it is a plant that will grow just about anywhere, and should be harvested while the stems are still green and the flowers are bright and white. It more or less dries by itself hung upside down or placed upright in a vase. Sea lavender purchased from the florist or a market stall during the summer is usually ready dried, or well on the way. It is frequently considerably cheaper than the sea lavender wrapped in cellophane and sold dried a month later in the dried flower shop.

To purchase dried

Like statice, dyed sea lavender can be lurid so take care when purchasing. The white, the softer pastel colours and some of the greens are safer bets. The dyed dark green statice is also useful.

Avena sativa (Oats)

Oats are inexpensive and easy to grow or buy.

To grow or to purchase fresh

Avena seed can be purchased from specialist seed merchants and should be harvested early to retain the soft green colour. When the oats turn to an oatmeal colour they can be used to effect in autumn designs.

To purchase dried

It is advisable to purchase oats that are protected by a cellophane wrap as the tips are easily damaged. Do check the colour has not faded.

Panicum miliaceum (Millet)

Although millet is technically a grass it looks so good in arrangements that it has to have an entry of its own. The stem is flexible when dried – sometimes too flexible – but the effect it gives is soft and flowing. It is excellent for creating the skeleton of a design giving lightness and grace.

To grow or to purchase fresh

Millet seeds can be purchased from a seed catalogue or a large garden centre and then planted in groups in the garden. It should be picked, as all grasses, when the sheath comes away from the flowering head, but before the seeds have had time to ripen. It can be dried flat on newspaper which will absorb any moisture.

To purchase dried

As with the other cereals and grasses, remember to check the colour has not faded.

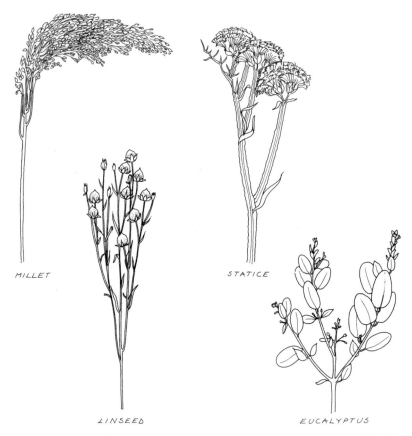

MILLET

STATICE

LINSEED

EUCALYPTUS

Linum usitatissimum (Linseed or common flax)

The small rounded seedheads of linseed are displayed on numerous branches from the main stem. They have strong sturdy stems and create a light but dense outline quickly, efficiently and effectively.

To grow or to purchase fresh

Although it is easy to find seed packets labelled linseed or flax you need to find a packet that says *Linum usitatissimum,* for it is the agricultural linseed, with its brilliant blue flowers, that produces those wonderful seedheads. If you are unable to find the seed in your garden centre, contact a specialist seed merchant. *Linum usitatissimum* can be sown directly into the soil in a sunny spot in the spring and left to produce flowers followed by the seedheads. These should be cut as soon as the green seedheads have formed, rather than waiting until they have turned yellow. Hang them up to dry and after a few weeks rub a seedhead between your fingers to check that they are completely dry.

To purchase dried

As with all green foliage and seedheads the colour needs to be fresh and lively. Check that the heads are not tangled together as they could easily get damaged.

Limonium sinuatum syn. Statice sinuatum (Statice)

Statice adds bright colour to arrangements but is often over-used and allowed to stay even when faded and way past its due date. Always replace tired statice. The brighter coloured statice is best used as a filler or to give colour accents rather than to create an outline. Statice is very useful because:

- During the summer months it can be purchased fresh from many market stalls and florists throughout the country.
- It is easy to dry by the hang dried method.
- The colour is retained extremely well.

To grow or to purchase fresh

Statice can easily be grown in the garden from seed. It is important to ensure that the flowers are open before cutting because once cut, the flowers will not continue to develop even if placed in water.

To purchase dried

Care must be taken when buying dried statice that the bunches have not been stored in too dry an atmosphere as many of the individual flowers will then drop out of the packaging when it is opened. Statice is extremely susceptible to dropping, especially when the atmosphere is too dry. Check to see that all the heads are full of flowers. Yellow statice is particularly vulnerable. Turn the bunch upside down to see how much drops before you buy it, but do this very gently as careless handling will soon damage the flowers. The colour of the white, blue and yellow statice should be strong, but the natural pink and peach statice always appear muted. Statice is sometimes dyed and can be lurid so it needs to be used with care.

Eucalyptus (S) (The gum tree)

Depending on the type, eucalyptus can be classified as line or branching material. Because it has interest down the full length of the stem, is flexible and is a soft grey-green colour it is extremely useful in dried flower work for creating the outline of a design. Eucalyptus is one of the few foliages which is not too brittle to use when it has been hang dried. It responds brilliantly to the glycerine treatment to which dye can be added so that colour and flexibility are retained. Appendix 2 describes this method of preservation in full.

To grow or to purchase fresh

There are many varieties available but choose one that has round, rather than long, leaves. The variety 'Stewartiana' has excellent rounded leaves on a robust stem, the ideal size for many arrangements. The variety 'Gunii' will produce lots of small rounded leaves but it must be pruned extremely hard. Whether pruned from the tree in the garden or purchased from the florist the stems of the eucalyptus should be fresh and strong when dried. If you try to hang dry eucalpytus which has been out of water for a long time the leaves will drop quickly, so if purchasing eucalyptus do ensure that it is fresh and not on the point of drying out. You will be able to tell if it is not fresh because many of the leaves will drop off when you pick it up. The fresher it is the more robust it will be when dried.

To purchase dried

Eucalyptus has usually been treated with glycerine and is consequently expensive. It is, however, a very easy and effective material to use.

—————— Line plant material ——————

LAVENDER

LAVENDULA STOECHAS

AMARANTHUS

LARKSPUR

Lavandula (Lavender)

Dried lavender can be expensive to buy, yet one plant in a tub, window box or in well drained soil in a sunny spot in the garden can repay its cost many times over. It is useful because it:

● is easy to grow;
● is easy to take cuttings;
● is easy to dry;
● is fragrant;
● can be used singly for small designs or bunched for larger ones.

To grow or to purchase fresh

The classification of lavender is rather complicated. To simplify it for dried flower purposes lavender can be termed English or French.

Under the heading 'English' lavender there are many varieties. The Old English Lavender has a wonderful fragrance but has a soft grey colour which can look rather sad and faded. Other English lavenders have a strong blue colour and are most effective in dried flower work. The varieties *Lavandula angustifolia* 'Hidcote' and *Lavandula angustifolia* 'Munstead' are excellent. Although many of the French lavenders are also effective when dried, avoid growing from the range *Lavendula stoechas*, which is easily recognisable by the tufts of purple bracts that persist after the flowers have faded. The bees love this early flowering lavender, and it is charming in the garden, but it loses a lot of its impact once dried.

Lavender will spread and flower each year, although after four or five years the mother plant can get rather straggly. Trim lightly every year and remove any old flowers that have escaped the drying process. You can regenerate it by taking your own cuttings to have a continuous supply. Pull off a non-flowering side shoot with a heel, that is with a small piece of the main stem. Trim off the bottom leaves with a sharp knife and push the stem end into the ground. If you have a heavy soil mix in a little sand first. Avoid taking cuttings during a long dry spell or when the plant is in full flower.

Pick your home-grown lavender before the flowers are fully open and hang it upside-down to dry.

To purchase dried

If lavender has been picked at full flowering it will quickly drop. Gently turn the bunch upside-down and see how much drops. Buy Old English lavender for fragrance and the deep-blue lavender for colour. According to the variety the length of stem varies considerably as does the amount of lavender down each stem. Choose lavender that suits your purpose, i.e. a small neat spike for smaller designs, longer, fuller stems for larger arrangements. The size of the bunches often varies, so measure the cost against the size of the bunch.

Amaranthus hypochondriacus (S) (Prince's feather)

The upright variety of amaranthus, not the drooping variety known as *Amaranthus caudatus* or Love-lies-Bleeding, is particularly useful. It is widely available in green or burgundy.

To grow or to purchase fresh

Amaranthus is extremely easy to grow from seed and can self-seed from one year to the next. Flowers should be cut when they are fully developed. Alternatively, they can be purchased fresh from a florist in late summer and hung up to dry.

To purchase dried

Amaranthus is relatively robust and the green variety retains freshness of colour particularly well. However, do check when purchasing that it has been harvested at the correct time and that the flowers have opened up to the tip.

Delphinium consolida (Larkspur)

Larkspur is the annual relative of the perennial delphinium. Both larkspur and delphinium retain colour extremely well once dried. Because of their long stems they are useful in large arrangements. Larkspur can be grown or purchased in white, pink, blue and mauve. Much of the colour is retained once dried.

To grow or to purchase fresh

Sow a packet of seeds where you wish the flowers to grow, following the instructions on the packet, and you will have flowers through late summer and early autumn. Harvest when most of the flowers are fully out and the top flowers of the spike are showing colour.

To purchase dried

When purchasing check that the colour is strong. Although the colour lasts well, the previous year's stock is not going to have the same intensity of colour. There should be some colour showing on most of the flower tips. Check that the flowers are densely packed up the stem. The longer the flowering part of the stem, the better the value as each stem can be broken down into smaller pieces. The lower flowers can be removed to create a longer stem and added to a pot pourri or used to hide the foam inside a glass container. Remove the topmost tips if these flowers are undeveloped and look faded.

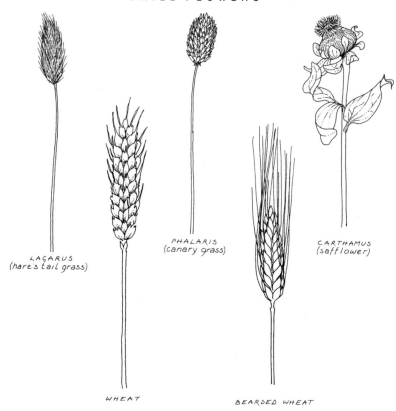

LAGARUS
(hare's tail grass)

PHALARIS
(canary grass)

CARTHAMUS
(safflower)

WHEAT

BEARDED WHEAT

Lagurus ovatus and Phalaris canariensis (Hare's tail grass and Canary grass)

These ornamental grasses are most attractive and are two of the most commonly used in dried flower work. Hare's tail is easily distinguished by its soft, fluffy head. Canary grass has oval flower-heads with green veins. Both grasses are frequently dyed but their natural soft colouring is ideal for adding to traditional designs. In large designs they need to be grouped. Many grasses, not just hare's tail and Canary, give a lightness and free-flowing movement to traditional dried flower designs. The stems remain semi-flexible when dried and many can be placed to fall gently over the rim of a container, thus softening the design. If you use a lot of grasses it usually gives an informal feel to a design, ideal for the kitchen, but perhaps less effective in a more formal room.

To grow or to purchase fresh

All grasses are more attractive picked early in the season before they are too ripe and have dispersed their seeds. There is no need to hang them upside-down to dry. Just leave them on a sheet of newspaper or upright in a container. The greener the stems are when picked – which is earlier rather than later in the season – the greener they will be when dried. Alternatively, buy a packet of mixed seeds and follow the instructions on the packet. Wild grasses, particularly those that grow by the sea, are useful in dried flower designs. Meadow and wayside grasses also dry well. Some florists now sell more unusual grasses, such as a commercial version of sticky 'Goose Grass', which looks most effective when fresh and green.

To purchase dried

Various grasses can be purchased from the dried flower specialist. Oatmeal coloured grasses always seem to give a slightly 'tired' look to an arrangement so try to find new stock that is a fresh green colour. Grasses can be purchased dyed in a vast array of colours and can look most effective.

Triticum aestivum (Wheat)

Wheat is useful in continental designs because of its straight stem, and in larger traditional designs, but it is rather stiff in smaller arrangements. Wheat sheaves can be easily made by tying a couple of bunches tightly together as a central core and then splaying a third bunch around them. This should be kept in place by tying it in high up, just under the ears, and then twisting so that they form a spiral over the core. A raffia plait or hessian ribbon can be used as a decorative feature. *Triticum durum* has long awns and is most attractive.

Wheat can be used to create a change of movement and to add interest to floral rings, swags and garlands. It is usually inexpensive to purchase.

To grow or to purchase fresh

If you have difficulty finding wheat seed you can always try sowing mixed chicken corn. However, once the harvest is in, most farmers would not be adverse to having their gleanings collected and put to good use, but do ask them first. Wheat should be collected as soon as the harvest is in before it becomes too oatmeal in colour. Wheat can be placed upright in a container or laid flat on newspaper to dry.

To purchase dried

Wheat is an inexpensive purchase. Unless used for Harvest or Thanksgiving, try to find wheat that is a soft green colour. Moths and mice both seem to be particularly partial to wheat, the riper the better, so if you see that 'ears' are missing you may well fear the worst!

Carthamus tinctorius (Safflower or Saffron thistle)

Carthamus can be all green or have the more familiar orange, yellow or cream thistle-like flowers which develop later. It is still grown today for its yellow dye. In an autumnal arrangement, the warm orange and yellow tones look good but can be difficult to mix with more distant colours on the colour wheel, such as pink. Because of the strong interest down the stem carthamus is marvellous as a filler, disguising bare stems and giving bulk to the design. In certain designs carthamus can be used as a focal flower.

To grow or to purchase fresh

Carthamus is easily grown in the garden from seed sown in the spring. If all green carthamus is desired cut the stems when the buds are full, but just before the flower bursts. Harvest the orange or yellow flowers when one or two have developed on each stem. This means that some of the flowers on the stem will still be in the green bud stage, but if you wait too long for more flowers to open the first ones may well be past their best. Hang dry as quickly as possible.

To purchase dried

Fresh stock which has been harvested correctly has a fresh green colour. Old stock will have faded to a pale yellow-green which is not nearly as attractive.

—————— Focal plant material ——————

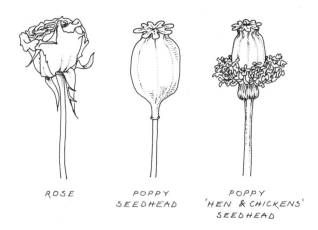

ROSE

POPPY
SEEDHEAD

POPPY
'HEN & CHICKENS'
SEEDHEAD

Rosa (S) (Rose)

A flower arrangement is set apart from the stereotyped masses by the inclusion of roses. Twelve roses in a medium-sized arrangement can give a strength of colour and beauty of form that is hard to beat. Roses can be added to any design and always give a hint of luxury.

To grow or to purchase fresh

It is extremely easy to dry roses following the hang drying method. Roses can be dried from the garden, the market stall or the florist when they are inexpensive and plentiful during the summer months. It is rare that you will use long stemmed roses as the proportion of dried stem to head is too great. Short-stemmed roses are always cheaper than their taller relations so there is no need to buy longer lengths than will be needed in your design.

It is said that if you add a teaspoon of sugar to the water containing the rose the night before you dry it, the colour will be more intense when dried. Try it!

Do remember that all flowers shrink in volume once dried. This can be particularly disappointing with dried roses. Avoid inexpensive buys of small roses unless small arrangements are your aim. Full garden roses dry extremely well, but are much more expensive to purchase partly because their fullness means they are more susceptible to damage. Pick them and allow them to develop fully in a vase so their heads are dry just before their point of perfection. Then follow the instructions in Appendix 1. Do not attempt to dry roses that are in any way mouldy. If roses have been kept tightly wrapped in cellophane for too long they could well have started to develop mould in the centre of each flower. If so they will shatter easily once dried.

To purchase dried

Dried roses are usually sold in twenties. If sold in smaller amounts the price should be correspondingly less. If the bunches have been handled carelessly by the retailer or a clumsy customer, several heads may have broken off. One or two heads missing is acceptable but beware if more are missing. The foliage of a dried rose will never be as vibrant a green as its fresh counterpart. It does, however, need to have a good green colour, rather than a stale yellow one. Roses that have been in stock for a long time acquire a yellowish-brown appearance up the side of the head, even though the flat head often retains its stronger colour, so be sure to examine potential purchases carefully. Roses vary quite substantially in price. Those which grow most easily and dry with good colour retention are usually slightly cheaper. More unusual varieties such as the bi-coloured roses such as 'Pasa Doble' and 'La Minuet' are often more expensive. Garden roses, which have a fuller shape, are considerably more expensive.

Papaver (S) (Poppy seedheads)

Poppy seedheads can be added to just about any arrangement. *Papaver Somniferum* 'Gigantium' gives enormous seedheads and *Papaver Somniferum* 'Minimum' produces tiny seedheads; most useful in miniature designs. The Shirley poppy *Papaver rhoeas* has a slightly narrower form. There are many more from which to choose to give a wide variety of size and form. All varieties are invaluable because of their smooth texture and bold form.

To grow or to purchase fresh

A packet of poppy seeds will grow just about anywhere. If you have the space buy a few packets of seeds to produce seedheads of different sizes. The seeds can be scattered between shrubs, over window boxes or in tubs. Pick your crop shortly after the petals have fallen otherwise the insects will get there first. The poppy seedheads can be hung upside down to dry, but put paper bags over the heads to catch the seeds which otherwise drop everywhere. Be sure you put ventilation holes in the bags because the lack of air circulation will encourage a grey mould called *botrytis* to grow. Poppy seedheads can simply be put upright in an empty container to dry as the stem is strong. Take the poppies outside at regular intervals and shake the heads over an area where you would like to see the flowers growing the following year.

To purchase dried

When purchasing dried poppy seedheads it is difficult to go wrong. They are often available in three sizes:

- mini
- standard
- giant

The standard size is probably the most useful and the most easy to find. It is now possible to buy a variety called 'Hen and Chickens' – a charmingly different variety which gives excitement to any design.

Poppy seedheads are generally easier to see if the stems are reasonably straight, particularly if you are interested in the modern designs. When purchasing you should check that they have not been nibbled or squashed, and be aware that the giant size is expensive but most attractive. If you are interested in the variety 'Hen and Chickens', ensure that the chickens round the hen are well-formed and not broken.

Nigella damascena (S) (Love-in-a-mist)

The subtle neutral pinkish colouring and different shape of the feathery inflated seedhead means that nigella can be added to any arrangement to give interest. They look lovely sprayed gold in Christmas designs.

To grow or to purchase fresh

Although nigella is not the easiest flower to grow from seed it will, if the soil is left relatively undisturbed, self seed and you will have a yearly supply from one packet of seeds. After the petals have fallen, allow the seedheads to develop fully before hanging upside down to dry. If purchased, the seedheads can be allowed to develop in situ after the petals have fallen. The seeds of more unusual varieties of nigella may be harder to find.

To purchase dried

Nigella damascena is widely available. Some bunches have very definite pink markings. Many outlets now stock *Nigella orientalis* which has an interesting geometric shape with a smooth ridged texture.

When purchasing take care that the seedheads are not straw-coloured, for this will mean that it is old stock or has been stored in strong sunlight. Also ensure that the seedheads of *Nigella damascena* are plump and not flattened, and that *Nigella orientalis* has a good green colouring.

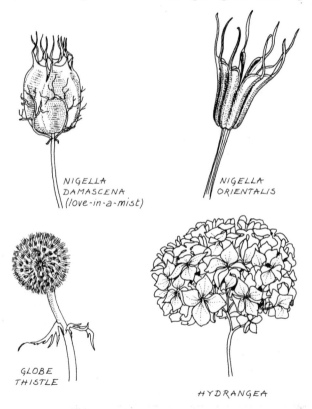

NIGELLA
DAMASCENA
(love-in-a-mist)

NIGELLA
ORIENTALIS

GLOBE
THISTLE

HYDRANGEA

Echinops ritro (S) (Globe thistle)

Although close examination shows the globe thistle to be rough, the overall impression is of a smooth round ball. The spiky steel-blue heads are an exciting addition to almost any design.

To grow or to purchase fresh

It is incredibly easy to grow the globe thistle in the garden. It is a perennial that will flower year after year with little attention. It only needs to be cut back to the ground each autumn. The stems are so sturdy that the thistles can be picked and arranged where they will dry. Pick and dry them before they are mature and the small flowers at the end of each spike have developed. Choose a variety with a strong blue colouring as the colour will eventually fade.

To purchase dried

If purchased in the shops the globe thistle can be expensive. This is because the seedhead, by virtue of its shape and delicacy, is easily spoiled. Those that have been crushed cannot be repaired. Globe thistles that have a strong steel-blue colour rather than a paler tint and are smaller rather than larger in size are the best to buy. Sometimes they have been dipped in dye but the resultant colour is often a rather harsh blue.

Hydrangea

Hydrangeas are invaluable for three reasons:

- Small pieces from the main floret can be used to hide foam.
- Their bold, large form is ideal in large arrangements.
- Wonderful topiary trees can be simply and easily made using hydrangea.

To grow or to purchase fresh

A hydrangea bush can easily be grown in a pot but care must be taken that it is watered frequently until well established. It is strongly recommended that if you do not have a hydrangea bush you should either:

- locate one in the garden of a generous friend, neighbour or relative; or

- buy one and plant it ready for cropping the following year.

The mop headed hydrangeas that have a globular appearance are more useful than the lacecaps. Whatever colour you buy, it may well change according to the make up of your soil. Pink flowers will turn bluer in acid soil and blue flowers will turn pinker in alkaline soil. It is easy to buy kits to test the acidity of your soil from the garden centre. You can also buy a 'blueing' agent to add to the soil which will change the colour of hydrangeas. It generally has more effect on plants in tubs. An alternative is to add used tea leaves to alkaline soils as the tannic acid can help increase the acidity.

It does not really matter what colour your hydrangeas are – in fact the wider the range of colour you can amass the better.

Experience will tell you when your hydrangeas are ready for cutting. The colour will subtly change late in the year, before the first heavy frosts. The flower-heads will then feel firm and papery to the touch. Only take about one third of the flowers from a hydrangea bush as the flowers grow on the previous year's wood. If you take all the flowers you will have none the next year.

Place the freshly cut stem in soaked wet foam or in several inches of water. Allow the hydrangea to dry out slowly. Do not add extra water to the vase or foam. This slow method of drying out will prevent the bracts, which surround the tiny inner flowers, from curling tightly. Some people believe that one variety or colour dries better than another, but it is very much a personal experience. Few florists sell hydrangeas and if they do the quality is rarely adequate for drying.

To purchase dried

This is a flower-head that is far better found in gardens than in shops. Growers find it difficult to meet the demand for quality blooms. They are easily damaged in transit. The colour is often faded and the price alone prohibits purchase. In the autumn many bazaars and church fetes sell them cheaply. This is the time to buy in your supplies.

Helichrysum bracteatum (S) (Straw flower or Everlasting)

Helichrysums are probably the most commonly purchased dried flower and can be misused. If picked at the right time and used with discrimination they can look superb.

To grow or to purchase fresh

Helichrysum seeds are usually sold as half hardy annuals. This means they are meant to be sown indoors or in the greenhouse and transplanted outside after the fears of frost have gone. In mild climates there should be no danger of planting outside in May and picking until the first frosts. Alternatively, buy a couple of plants from the garden centre. If you keep picking the flowers each plant will produce an abundance of flowers.

Helichrysums in dried flower arrangements go dreadfully wrong when the flowers have been picked too late in their development. Look at the two flowers below, the one on the left was picked far too late and has blown. It is no longer a flower of beauty. The petals have turned backwards to expose an unattractive central disc. Straw flowers such as those on the right can be used to good effect.

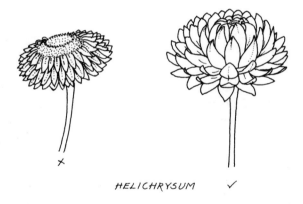

HELICHRYSUM

Straw flowers continue to mature and open even when cut. They can easily be purchased in the summer months from market stalls and florists. It is important that no part of the central disc is showing when they are picked.

The disadvantage of the helichrysum is that the stem is fragile once dried and you can be left with a bunch of dried heads with no stems. These can be used in pot pourri or have sticks wired or glued to the underneath of the flower. It is, however, much better to wire them while still fresh (see Appendix 5).

To purchase dried

- Only purchase if most of the flowers have not blown.
- Those that have been wired or had sticks attached will be more expensive. Wired stems are more useful as they can be flexed and angled at will. Unfortunately sticks are more commonly used as this is a cheaper manufacturing process.
- Dyed helichrysums are more expensive.
- *Helichrysums vestium* has a soft stem and a lax head and can be difficult to use.
- Helichrysum heads can be purchased loose or in packets. They are usually inexpensive purchased in this way. It is easy to glue the tip of a wire to the undersurface of the head.
- It is usually a better buy to purchase a bunch of only one colour, rather than mixed.

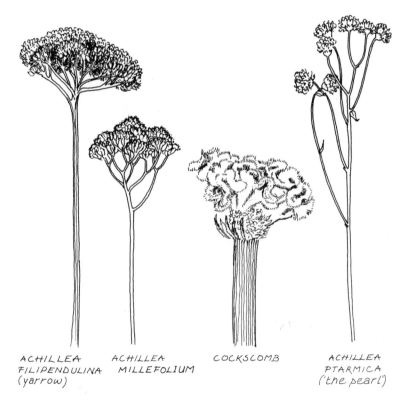

ACHILLEA FILIPENDULINA (yarrow)   ACHILLEA MILLEFOLIUM   COCKSCOMB   ACHILLEA PTARMICA ('the pearl')

Achillea

There are several varieties of achillea which are extremely useful.

Achillea filipendulina has large flat deep yellow strong heads which retain their colour exceptionally well. Its strong sturdy stem means it can be arranged and left in situ to dry.

Achillea millefolium, commonly known as yarrow, has large flat heads of varying soft shades of salmon, yellow, white and lilac. The heads are generally not as large or as rigid as those of *Achillea filipendulina*. They are wonderful for filling out large arrangements.

Achillea ptarmica, 'The Pearl', commonly known as sneezewort, has a very different appearance from the *Achillea filipendulina* and *Achillea millefolium*. The flowers retain their white-cream colour well. The stems are strong and the light colouring of the flowers gives a lift to many arrangements.

To grow or to purchase fresh

Achilleas are easily grown perennials producing flowers year after year. The yellow variety keeps its colour particularly well.

Achillea can be found fresh in many flower shops during the summer and autumn months. The colours of the *Achillea millefolium* tend to soften during the dying process and are most attractive. This variety needs to be harvested in late summer when the flowering stems, which are not as strong as those of *Achillea filipendulina*, have strengthened and the heads are firm to the touch. The wild yarrow is very similar but the stems are weaker.

To purchase dried

Achillea filipendulina is easily found. The flowers usually have very long stems. Check that the heads have not been crushed. It is often available dyed in a wide range of colours, but these are usually far more expensive.

The 'Pearl' should be a clear cream colour. It should be picked when fully out but before any rain. It is only brown when it has been harvested too late. The colour dulls eventually with keeping.

Celosia (S) (Cockscomb)

Celosia has a dense velvety texture. Its head of sumptuous colour gives impact and richness to any design.

To grow or to purchase fresh

Celosia is not one of the easiest flowers to grow in the garden, making it the one exception to easily grown flowers and seedheads mentioned in this chapter. It really needs to be grown under glass. However, it can easily be purchased during the summer months from good florists. Choose bunches with good colour. Simply hang upside-down to dry.

To purchase dried

Red, pink and yellow celosia should have a good colour intensity. Some of the stems can be very thick and difficult to insert into a small amount of foam.

Paeonia (Peony)

Peonies are like roses in that they give a richness to any design.

To grow or to purchase fresh

If you do not possess a peony bush, purchasing one can only be a good investment but you may have to wait a few years for it to bear flowers. They grow easily in tubs on patios or in the garden and are only temperamental if moved. Red, deep pink and white peonies keep their colour well, but the pale pink peony seems to fade rather quickly. Enjoy peonies as fresh flowers until the flower has opened to show all its petals but is not past its peak. Peonies shrink a good deal during the drying process. Fresh peonies are now sold in many florists shops during May and June.

To purchase dried

As pale pink peonies seem to fade rather quickly buy those with stronger rather than weaker colour. White peonies retain their colour as well, if not better, than any other white flower. Check the price – they can be ferociously expensive but they are worth it.

5

ADDITIONAL ___ MATERIAL

There is a wide variety of both natural and artificial material that can be added to designs to provide contrast in texture, shape and colour. Techniques today are so sophisticated that it can be hard to distinguish the artificial from its natural counterpart.

———— Natural material ————

Moss

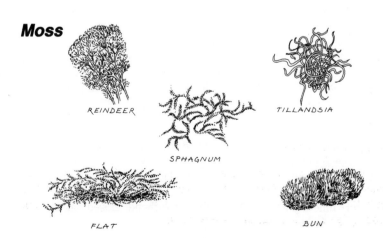

REINDEER

SPHAGNUM

TILLANDSIA

FLAT

BUN

Moss is an important component of dried flower work. It can be used to conceal the foam or other mechanics, give textural interest or used in conjunction with wire netting to form a base into which stems can be inserted. There are several types of moss available.

Reindeer moss (Iceland moss, lichen moss)

Reindeer moss in its natural state grows in Scotland, Finland and other locations where there are cold winters and extensive scrubland. It can be easily purchased. Dyed reindeer moss is treated with a glycerine solution so that it will not dry out and become brittle. Untreated moss can become stiff and difficult to spread out. If it does, dip it in water, squeeze out as much moisture as you can and it will fluff out and become flexible and easy to use. Brightly dyed mosses can be useful when creating colourful topiary trees, but the more natural green and creams are generally a much better buy. When packaged in plastic bags the moss spreads to fill the space available. Therefore you should always check the weight of the bag against the cost if you are purchasing moss in this way.

Tillandsia moss (Spanish moss)

This moss is not so readily available, but is worth the search as it is exciting in designs even though at first sight it looks like a devastated bird's nest or straggly seaweed. It is, in fact, an air plant, *Tillandsia usenoides*. Added to your work it gives a softness and looseness that is refreshingly natural. It is usually sold in neutral colours – green and cream. It is more expensive than reindeer moss, but a little goes a long way.

Spagnum moss

This is a moss that can be acquired from most florists. It grows naturally in boggy land. It is cheaper than reindeer moss but as it dries out the colour and spring are lost. It is an ideal material to use to cover mechanics where little is going to be exposed. It can be tightly packed inside wire netting shapes to create the base for floral rings, garlands and topiary trees. Tease out the moss and remove any twigs or pieces of debris. It is much easier to use if it is slightly damp but obviously too much moisture with dried flowers is not advisable. Spagnum moss can be kept for a long time if you keep it in a dark, polythene, closed bag in a cool place.

Bun moss

Bun moss is rather like a soft round green cushion. Unlike spagnum moss it has an earth back. It is sold commercially but is not always easy to find. Bun moss is often seen growing in thick rounded clumps on paths and roofs. It pulls away easily, with or without the help of a knife. It is not suitable for all dried flower work as it is difficult for stems to penetrate but wires can easily be pushed through. Some of the earth backing can be removed with a knife. Bun moss can be used to decorate the bases of topiary trees, or incorporated into modern designs to give strong textural contrast.

Flat moss (carpet moss)

This is a thin spongy moss, with an earth back, that grows on lawns, usually when you do not want it to! It can be purchased in large flat pieces from specialist shops. It is used to cover mechanics, of, say, wire netting, to give a smooth flat finish. It can be used for sculptured trees (see Figure 16 in the colour section) or for covering animals made from wire netting and spagnum moss.

Fruit

Many small fruits can be successfully dried if kept over several weeks in a warm airing cupboard or left on a sunny window ledge. Limes and small lemons are particularly suitable.

Pomegranates

Pomegranates are superb focal features of floral rings, swags and garlands. They are expensive to buy commercially dried. To prepare them yourself is simple. When you have bought the pomegranates leave them for a few days to harden a little so that they are reasonably firm to the touch. Cut off the flat end of the pomegranate with a serrated knife. Scoop out all the seeds with a small-headed spoon. Place the pomegranate in a warm oven for about 10 minutes to dry out. Store for several days until all the remaining moisture has evaporated. Place a blob of strong glue on the inside and press a length of garden or kebab stick, or heavy gauge wire in place. Hold until the glue sets.

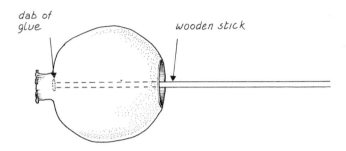

Orange slices

Again these are expensive to buy but easy to make yourself. Place thin, but even, slices of orange on a baking sheet that has been covered with absorbent kitchen towels. Put the tray in a very low oven for several hours and check regularly to see that they are not going brown. The bottom of an Aga is ideal. Alternatively, dry them in a microwave.

Once the slices are dry you can paint them with a clear varnish, but this is not essential. The slices can be used to decorate the top of a container or in swags, garlands or floral rings. Simply pass a medium gauge wire through the pith and twist as close to the peel as possible. The slices can then be easily inserted into your design.

Apple slices

Apple slices look attractive threaded into garlands, made into floral rings or added to an autumnal basket arrangement. Use firm apples with a green or red skin. Cut into thin slices and coat with a mixture of lemon juice and water. This will minimize browning. Put into a low oven, the bottom of an Aga is, again, ideal, and remove before they turn brown. Courgettes, aubergines and other fruits and vegetables can also be dried following this method.

Freeze-dried flowers, fruit and vegetables

Freeze-drying removes the moisture content from flowers, fruits and vegetables. The great advantage of this process is that it preserves the perfect form and colour of the fruit or vegetable, even those which it would be impossible to preserve successfully by any other method, for example strawberries and kiwi fruit. The disadvantage is that this process of preservation has to be done commercially as very expensive equipment is involved. Freeze-dried materials are not cheap to buy, but they are very easy to use in floral rings and garlands as they are very light and the effect is superb. A wooden stick or wire can easily be inserted into the fruit or vegetable to hold them in place. This is also an excellent way of preserving flowers that would lose much of their interest if dried by hanging. Freeze-dried parrot tulips and lilies can be indistinguishable from the fresh flower. If they are hang-dried they appear limp and lose their three-dimensional form.

Cinnamon sticks

Cinnamon sticks give a wonderful fragrance. They also give a rich smooth texture, an ideal contrast to the rough texture of many dried flowers. Their linear shape can give exciting impact to many designs. Their cost often relates to their packaging, so avoid paying for expensive bottles by searching for them in health food shops where they can be bought by the gram or ounce. Try to buy whole ones and if you need to make them smaller, use a serrated knife or scissors to minimise crumbling and waste. Cinnamon sticks can be used in twos or threes for impact. Use a medium gauge wire to bind them together. Wrap it round once and then twist. The wire can be covered by thin ribbon, raffia, decorative rope, gold thread or a natural jute garden twine. You can also decorate the cinnamon by threading a wire through a length of gold or silver bullion wire available from some market stalls, department stores and mail order companies. The decorated wire is then wound round the piece of cinnamon and the ends twisted together to form a stem which should be stem-taped. Bullion wire can also be used to decorate star anise and poppy seedheads.

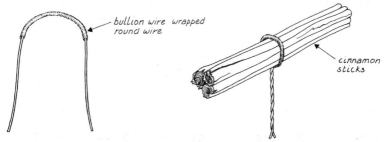

bullion wire wrapped round wire

cinnamon sticks

Exotica

Exotica is a word that refers to plant material that originates in 'exotic' parts, such as Australia and South America. Examples are giant seed-pods, spathes, cane cones, proteas, banksias, hoya leaves and bell cups. The arrangement in Figure 15 in the colour section uses only exotics and a few orange marigolds. As the colours are usually tints and tones of brown, strong emphasis has to be made exclusively of texture and form when using exotics. Some of the most commonly available exotics are:

Lotus seedheads

Lotus seedheads are superb for their texture and shape. They give excitement to any design and are used particularly when textural contrast is required. They can often be acquired in a mini form, useful for small designs, and in a larger form which is useful when the scale of the other components is greater. They look lovely sprayed gold in festive arrange-ments. They can be purchased on a stem but it is much cheaper simply to push a heavy-gauge wire or wooden stick into the base of the lotus seedhead, which is soft, and to add a dab of glue to keep it in place.

LOTUS SEEDHEAD

Mushrooms

Although there are many types of fungi that can be collected and dried in, for example, an airing cupboard, there are two main types of mushroom which can be bought commercially:

- golden mushrooms
- sponge mushrooms

When drying some varieties of mushroom in the home, they can get rather smelly.

Golden mushrooms

Golden mushrooms look as if they have been sculptured from wood. They have a small stalk which can be sharpened and inserted directly into the foam. Alternatively, the stem can be extended with a heavy length of wire or a stick. Golden mushrooms can usually be purchased in both a small or large form.

GOLDEN MUSHROOM

Sponge mushrooms

One side of sponge mushrooms is smooth and the other is grooved. Either side can be used according to the texture that is required. Commercially sold sponge mushrooms have sometimes been treated to give a bleached effect. Sticks or heavy wires can easily be glued to the side of the mushroom which will not be exposed.

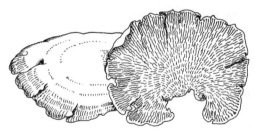

SPONGE MUSHROOM

Proteas and banksias

If you are planning a large, bold design proteas and banksias are dramatic and fill a lot of space. They belong to the same family, but whereas proteas come from South Africa, banksias come from Australia. Proteas and banksias are usually sold individually or occasionally in threes or fives. They can also be purchased fresh and are easily dried. The leaves, however, tend to turn brown. Mixed bunches of smaller members of the *Proteaceae* family can often be purchased fresh from florists.

Nails

Nails, or Preigos as they are officially called, are shown at the base of the arrangement on the front cover of the book. These amazing empty seed cases come from South America. They have a strong form and a smooth texture, ideal for including in many designs.

Nuts

There are many nuts suitable for inclusion in dried flower work. Walnuts are ideal as they possess a soft spot through which a wire or stick can easily be pushed. A dab of glue at the insertion point will ensure that the support does not come loose. Conkers are suitable as they can also easily be penetrated with a wire. Coat wired conkers with varnish to minimize shrivelling. Beech masts are attractive in small designs. A wire needs to be passed over the mast to give it a strong stem. Many have their own short stems which may be sufficient. Almonds, Brazil nuts and hazelnuts have to be drilled before a wire can be inserted.

Cones

All cones may be utilised depending on the scale of the design. Information on how to wire cones is in Appendix 5. The most easily found cones are perhaps those belonging to the pine. The larch tree produces small cones, grouped together on a small branch, that look delightful. The alder has tiny cones and catkins on delicate branches, which are useful for small-scale work.

Lichen and small twigs

Lichen-covered twigs and branches give a very natural feel to all styles of dried flower arrangements. Their delicate eau-de-nil colouring and interesting texture always give interest. Bare twigs incorporated into an arrangement give space within the design and a very natural feel. They are particularly effective in spring and winter designs. The design in Figure 20 in the colour section has used slim flexible stems that have been looped, held with stem tape and the free end inserted into the foam.

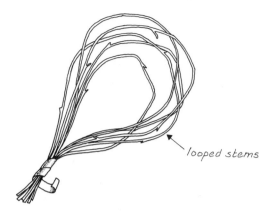

looped stems

Note

Always take from the countryside with discrimination so as not to alter the natural habitat in any way.

——————— Artificial additions ———————

Artificial plant material

In the last few years a profusion of artificial plant material has arrived in the shops that has transformed dried flower work. These flowers are made from many different substances – polyester, silk, fabric and even polystyrene! This book uses the term 'silk' flowers to cover all the different types of artificial flowers. Many of these flowers, seedheads and foliage are extremely beautiful. It is not possible to say how to choose the most beautiful artificial flowers but often price is a good guide line. If you want quality flowers they are usually just a little bit more expensive, but are worth that extra expense. Many of the larger department stores have fantastic displays of quality flowers from which to choose. Many of the silk flowers are so realistic that they can be added to dried or even fresh flowers without destroying the natural effect. Parchment flowers, made from the mulberry bush, are startlingly effective. Parchment and artificial flowers also have the advantage of being anti-allergenic and are more resistant to colour fading than dried flowers.

Unless you wish to create a large 'flowers in a vase' arrangement it is advisable to buy foliage, fruit and berries that can be split up into smaller units.

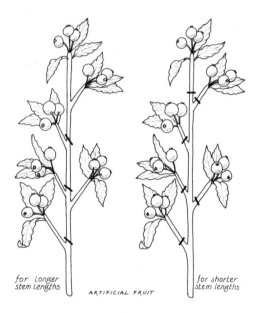

for longer
stem lengths

ARTIFICIAL FRUIT

for shorter
stem lengths

Wire cutters are ideal for this purpose but short bladed florists' scissors will cut thin wires easily.

If you buy a spray of fruit or apples which you wish to use on a floral ring do not throw away any of the artificial leaves which accompany the fruits. Get into the habit of keeping them. They can be used in a variety of designs, not necessarily in company with their fruit.

Because artificial plant material is wired it is a welcome addition to dried flower arranging. The wire enables it to be angled at will so that it can be:

- shown to advantage
- flexed to give space in the design
- bent over the rim of the container so that the plant material and the container harmonise well with each other.

Selected with care and used with discrimination artificial plant material is an invaluable aid to the flower arranger. It has come a long way from the plastic daffodils of the fifties.

Ribbons

There are so many beautiful ribbons on the market that can enhance your design. Paper ribbon is inexpensive, comes in a tight coil and once unravelled is stiff and holds a bow beautifully. To make the unravelling easier spray the ribbon lightly with water or uncoil with damp hands. A single knot tie gives a lovely effect. More complicated bows can easily be made. Wired ribbon can be expensive but has an opulence and richness of its own. It always looks good and holds its shape well.

Polypropylene ribbon, used by florists, is readily available from ribbon shops, flower club sales tables or from florists themselves. It is inexpensive and can be torn into narrow strips easily, without damaging the edges. It is rather shiny, however, so think carefully before adding too large a bow to an arrangement made entirely from natural plant material. It is sometimes worth paying a little more and using quality ribbon, especially if the components of your design have cost a lot of money.

Wired or paper bows

This method is particularly suitable for stiff paper bows. It also works with quality wired ribbon.

- Take a length of ribbon about 80 cm (2ft 6in).
- Find the central point and lightly crease.
- Decide on the size of the bow loops and bring both ends to the centre and cross them over.
- If you wish to make a fuller bow you could use a longer length of ribbon and make two or more loops on each side.
- Hold the centre of the bow firmly and wrap a wire or narrow piece of ribbon round and tie tightly.

Full bow made with polypropylene ribbon

- For a bow of approximately 12 cm (5 in) in diameter you will need about 1.5 m (5ft) of polypropylene ribbon. This ribbon can be torn into narrow strips quite easily without damaging the edges.
- Measure 12 cm (5 in) from the free end of the ribbon and roll the long end round and round this length, thus keeping the flattened roll 12 cm (5 in) long.
- When all the ribbon has been used, make a gentle crease across the centre by folding one end of the roll over to meet the other.
- Take a sharp pair of scissors and cut two shallow 'V's inwards, but stop short of the centre.
- Take a new, thinner piece of the ribbon, wrap it tightly round the centre of your bow and tie it, leaving two long loose ends.
- Place your fingers inside the bow and pull the innermost loop out, at the same time giving it a twist of 45 degrees.
- Repeat until all the loops have been drawn out, alternating the sides. Gently tease and twist your loops to form a uniform bow.
- The two long loose ends can be used to tie round a gift or a wedding bouquet.

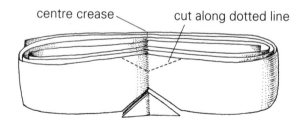

centre crease   cut along dotted line

Ribbon loops

Ribbon loops are simple to make and can be added to many designs to give contrast and an inexpensive alternative to flowers. Small loops can be added to topiary trees, larger ones to basket arrangements.

Make one, two or more loops of the required size. One of the loose ends can be brought upwards to be included with the loops. Wrap a length of florists' wire firmly round the bottom of the loops to make them secure.

6

——— EQUIPMENT ———

Most of the equipment needed for dried flower arranging is easily obtainable and not that expensive. One or two items do need to be searched for but they can be obtained from specialist shops and mail order companies. The names of some of these companies are given at the end of this book.

There are two specialist flower magazines in which companies that sell sundries advertise their wares. The first is the *Flower Arranger* magazine which is obtainable from all flower clubs throughout the country. Details of your local club are obtainable from NAFAS (The National Association of Flower Arrangement Societies of Great Britain). Alternatively, the magazine can be purchased directly from the publishers, Taylor Bloxham Ltd. The second magazine is *Flora International* which is obtainable from all good newsagents. Many garden centres sell a wide range of dried flowers and some sundries. Often florists will sell you the items you need.

Flower clubs are a magic world for those who are interested in flowers. Besides monthly demonstrations and teach-ins of fresh and dried flowers most flower clubs have sales tables where many of the items mentioned below may be purchased inexpensively.

Sundries

Dry foam

Dry floral foam is light, inexpensive and much tougher than the foam designed to take water and support fresh flower stems. Dry foam is usually grey in colour. There is also a less gritty, non-absorbent brown foam called Sahara which is harder than wet foam but not as hard as the dry foam. It is not as expensive as the grey foam and lighter stems can be inserted easily. If you have a propensity to take most stems in and out of the foam when arranging, or are using heavy stems, you would be advised to use the more resilient grey foam. Do take care after handling grey dry foam that you wash your hands as the smallest particle can cause serious eye irritation.

The most commonly purchased shape is the brick which is approximately $23 \times 11 \times 8$ cm ($9 \times 4.5 \times 3$ in). It can be easily cut with a sharp knife into the required shape. Cylinders of foam 5×8 cm (2×3 in) can also be purchased but only use these if you want to create a small round design. Avoid placing one on top of another to acquire height. It is better to use a single piece from a brick. Foam can be purchased in other shapes such as spheres, cones and circles.

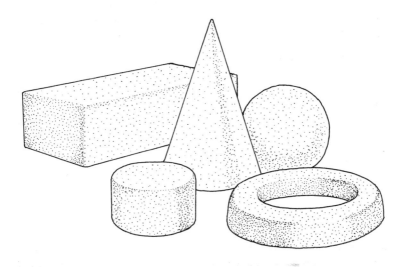

Although dry foam is extremely resilient, once there is a heavy network of holes you should throw the piece away and start anew. If your stems are soft consider using the softer wet foam designed for fresh stems. You will find it easier to use but it will break up more easily and is therefore not suitable for large, heavy stems.

An approximate amount of foam needed for each type of design is mentioned in the relevant chapter.

Containers

Dried flowers have a natural affinity to baskets but now that there is such a wealth of different plant materials available, evocative of every mood, there is no need to confine your flowers to baskets. Containers do not have to be waterproof. They can be of fine china, earthenware, in fact anything you wish to enhance with the addition of plant material. It can be a family heirloom or an old hat box unearthed at the local car boot sale.

Once you have decided on your container and have your foam you will need to fix one to the other so that your arrangement is stable. To do this you can use the following.

Florists' fix

This is similar to Plasticine, Blutack or chewing gum and indeed these can also be used. Fix is used when two hard surfaces need to be held together securely, but not permanently. A small piece needs to be worked and warmed in the hands before use to make it malleable. It can only be used to good effect when the surfaces to be held together are dry and dust free. (For this reason it is more difficult to use on baskets which usually have a rough, dusty surface which is more difficult to clean. For baskets use a thick wire bent in two and inserted up through the basket and the foam – see Chapter 7.) Fix is also used with frogs.

Frogs

A frog is an unusual name for a round plastic disc with four prongs.

It is used to secure foam to a container which has not been specifically

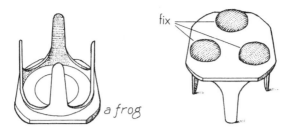

fix

a frog

designed to take its shape. A small knob of kneaded fix should be pressed on to the dry, dust-free undersurface of the frog. The frog and fix are then placed firmly in position in the container. The foam is then placed on the prongs of the frog. Frogs can be purchased in two sizes.

An alternative method of keeping foam in place is to use florists' tape. It can also be used in conjunction with a frog and fix to give extra security.

Florists' tape

This is a strong adhesive tape, purchased on a roll, which sticks firmly to foam. It is available in two widths. The narrower tape is usually sufficient for most arrangements. The ends should be strapped firmly across the top of the foam and well down the sides. Only use one or two lengths across the foam as too much tape will frustrate efforts to insert stems. The ends can be cut off once the plant material has been arranged. Once you are half way to completing your design you may be glad that you arranged this extra security.

Wire netting

Wire netting, or chicken-wire as it is also known, is used to:

- cover large pieces of foam, if you wish to give more strength when inserting a lot of stems.
- make bases for floral rings, topiary work, swags and garlands, in conjunction with spagnum moss.
- give support to flowers arranged in a vase.

Wire netting can be purchased in a variety of gauges. The 1.3 cm (0.5 in) gauge is generally the most useful size to buy if using for the first two points above.

If you wish to use it in a vase you will need the 5 cm (2 in) gauge. The amount you use depends to some extent on the size of the container and the thickness of the stems you wish to insert. A rough guide would be to cut a piece a little wider than the width of the opening and about three times the depth. Cut off the selvedge as this is stiff. Crumple the netting so that it forms approximately the same shape as the container. If you are using thick-stemmed branches, such as celosia, place a pinholder at the bottom of the base. Figure 12 in the colour section has been arranged in a vase containing only wire netting.

Green, plastic-coated wire netting is very flexible and easy on the hands but it is more expensive than the grey galvanized netting and not always as easy to find. If you buy a small roll it will work out much less expensive than small pre-packed amounts.

Candleholders

If you use dried flowers in a table centrepiece you may wish to include a candle. Specially designed plastic candleholders keep candles the most secure but are only designed for a standard traditional candle (such as in Figure 30 in the colour section). The design of the candleholder is such that it keeps the breaking up of the foam to the absolute minimum when the candles are inserted.

a candleholder

If the candle is too slim for the holder and wobbles, wedge it with newspaper or a little fix. Very slim candle tapers can be inserted directly into the foam. Do remember that dried plant material is extremely flammable and a lit candle should never be left alone.

Thick beeswax or church candles are lovely with dried flowers. Depending on their size you need to add lengths of heavy gauge wire, cocktail sticks or pieces of green garden stick to the sides of the candle and wrap florists' tape firmly around to keep them in place.

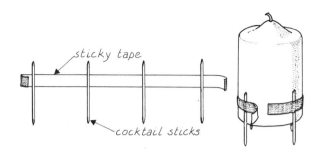

sticky tape

cocktail sticks

Scissors

Buying a good pair of scissors is expensive but essential. Household scissors will only frustrate you, and perhaps cut your fingers. Scissors need to have short blades, a serrated inner edge and, for preference, a hole to allow the easy cutting of thicker stems. They must also be easy to grasp. When buying a pair check if there is enough room for your fingers and thumb to fit comfortably in the handles. Good floral scissors will also enable you to cut thin wire without damaging the blades.

Glue guns

If you want to create floral rings and swags and other designs you will find that a glue gun is worth its weight in gold. A quality glue gun is an excellent investment. They can be easily obtained from DIY shops. There are many to choose from but do avoid the so called 'disposable' glue guns. They may be inexpensive but it is well worth paying more for one which is more durable.

Glue guns work when sticks of glue are fed into the gun which are then heated in the body of the gun producing a molten stream of hot glue which is a very efficient adhesive. The majority of guns are plugged into a socket and need only a few minutes before the glue will start to flow. Surfaces stick together in seconds, just like magic. The glue is strong and clear, and once you have used a glue gun its just like doing without the dishwasher – you cannot! The tiny threads of glue that might trail over your work can easily be pulled away without damage. The one disadvantage with the glue gun is that the glue burns if it lands on your hands – so take care. Low temperature glue guns are now widely available. These heat the glue to a lower temperature, greatly reducing the risk of burns.

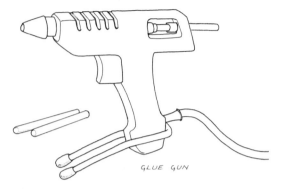

GLUE GUN

They are ideal for use on more delicate material but the adhesive quality is not quite as strong. It is a case of personal preference.

If you have a chance to try out a few glue guns consider the following:

• Compare the price of the glue sticks, the cost can vary enormously. Different glue guns take different glue sticks. Sometimes other sticks will fit your gun but it is not a good idea to use them as each type of gun will melt the stick at a different temperature. This means that if the wrong glue stick is used the glue will probably melt too quickly and will drip all over the place and be wasteful. On the other hand, you might have to push the trigger feverishly to acquire a mere drop – and that can be equally frustrating. Check how easily you can acquire the correct glue sticks. Low temperature glue guns usually use an oval glue stick to prevent the wrong glue being used.

• See how much dripping occurs (with the right glue stick). You may prefer to have a gun with a built in drip-tray.

• Has the gun been designed for continuous use or infrequent work? The price will vary accordingly but beware of buying a very cheap gun – it will not be a worthwhile investment.

• Is the trigger action easy to use. Do you have to apply a lot of pressure?

• The support stands are either at the front or back. See which suits you best. Check that the gun really does stay upright when on the stand.

Glues

If you do not have a glue gun there is a wealth of glues on the market from which to choose. For pressed flower work in particular PVA (polyvinyl acetate) glues are ideal. There are many brand names from which to choose, such as Marvin Medium, and they are all relatively inexpensive. They are water-based glues which are milky when liquid but dry clear. PVA glues can also be used for fixing dried and artificial plant material to floral rings or swags, but for large items a glue gun is easier to use. Bostik tube adhesives and UHU are multipurpose glues that work well.

Flower dyes

Carters of Blackburn has been producing flower dyes for many years. They are remarkably easy to use and the effect can be stunning. Simply follow the instructions on the bottle. There is a wide variety of colours that can be mixed together to achieve the required shade. The foliage (and flower-heads) are first dipped into a fixitive and then into the dye solution. When you first use these dyes, start with a weaker solution than is recommended on the bottle. Using dyes is an excellent way to revitalize faded flowers and to add more permanent, stronger colour to your arrangements. The only disadvantage is that the stems can also get covered in dye unless you are careful. Avoid getting the dyes on your clothes as they are obviously difficult to remove. If you are dipping grasses into dye you might need to dry them with a hairdryer to fluff them up.

An alternative way of dyeing your plant material is to add the dye to a glycerine mixture which the plant material will drink internally. This is a wonderful way of keeping your foliage flexible and green. Add a few drops of dye to the glycerine mixture and stir well before inserting your stems. Details on how to use a glycerine mixture are given in Appendix 2.

Cones and some strong seedheads can be dipped or left in a strong bleach solution to take the colour away and give interesting bleached white plant material.

Oasis and other companies have produced a wide range of spray paints specially formulated for dried flower work which are very effective. If you cannot find these, car spray paints also work well. Woolworths usually produce a top-class gold spray paint towards Christmas. Place the items to be sprayed in a large box to localise the spray and follow the instructions for use very carefully.

Always store dyes, bleach and spray paints out of the reach of children.

7

TRADITIONAL
——— FLOWER ———
DESIGNS

Traditional designs are composed of a mixture of flowers, seedheads and foliage, seemingly placed at random and flowing happily out of a basket, box or other container. All the stems appear to radiate from a single central point (see Chapter 1).

——————— The container ———————

Dried flowers look good not just in baskets but in glass vases, boxes, urns, washbasins, terracotta pots – in fact just about anything. So the first element you need to choose for this type of design is the container. Perhaps the most widely seen grouping of dried plant material is presented in a basket. For your first attempt, try using a small to medium sized basket or a container with a simple shape. Some baskets are easier to fill than others. The choice is enormous. They can be found at market stalls or department stores, and there is usually a plentiful supply at autumn bazaars for tens of pence.

The easiest baskets to fill successfully are those that:

- have a regular shape, i.e. baskets with a symmetrical shape that are meant to be viewed all round rather than positioned against a wall or fireplace which might have a raised back. The basket could be oval, round, or rectangular or square.
- have a handle that links the two short sides rather than the two longer sides. Baskets without handles can sometimes be easier to use.
- have enough space between the handle and the basket to allow the flowers to be more important than the basket, without the handle being totally hidden.

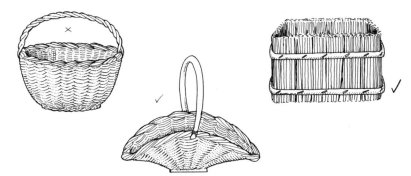

- have a natural or subtle colour. Light-coloured baskets give a fresh spring look and the darker wicker always enhances dried flowers. Lightly printed baskets can give an interesting extra dimension to your design, but brightly coloured and heavily printed baskets can be more difficult to fill effectively.

Once you have chosen your container you have to insert the foam.

The foam

The size and shape of the foam you use is important. The piece of foam needs to be:

- large enough to take all the stems but no larger. If the piece used is too big all your efforts to produce a natural design, incorporating space, will be thwarted by concern to cover all the foam. Your work would become rigid and over-filled. In a low container such as a

basket or bowl approximately one-third of the internal area of the container should be filled with foam. The shape of the foam should repeat the shape of the container, i.e. a roundish piece in a round container and an oval or rectangular piece in a rectangular container.
- tall enough to rise about 2.5 cm (1 in) above the rim of a small container, 5 cms (2 in) above the rim of a medium sized one and perhaps 7.5 cm (3 in) above a large one.

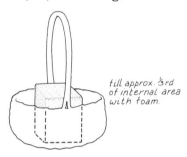

fill approx. ⅓rd
of internal area
with foam.

- chamfered around the edges. This means cutting away the sharp edges of the foam to give it a softer shape and greater surface area into which stems can be inserted.

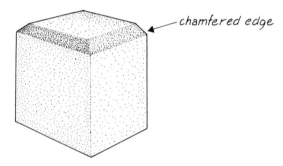

chamfered edge

The foam needs to be securely fixed into the container. If the foam is merely placed on the base of the basket you would have a moving flower arrangement. However, with most baskets it is easy to make the foam secure. Most basketry is woven sufficiently loosely for a long heavy wire (30 cm (11.5 in)) to be doubled and inserted through the bottom of the basket and through the foam. The two ends that protrude are then turned back into the foam. For pots, bowls and other solid containers, however, you will need to use a frog and fix. Florists' tape may be used to give additional security (see page 67).

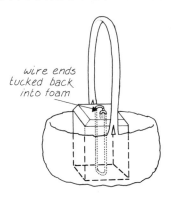

wire ends
tucked back
into foam

—— Material for covering the foam ——

You now need to choose a material for hiding the foam. Dried flower work differs from fresh flower work in that there is no lush green foliage to hide the mechanics. Most dried foliage is brittle and of restricted use.

Foam that is not covered before you start will result in a stiff, cluttered design. You will use more flowers for less effect. Fortunately there are solutions.

Moss

Reindeer moss is an ideal material for covering foam. As explained in Chapter 5 this can be purchased from florists, garden centres or specialist mail order companies.

Spagnum moss has the advantage of being readily available from most florists. It is cheaper than reindeer moss but loses its colour and flexibility when it dries out. It tends to disintegrate.

Hydrangea

If you have access to a hydrangea bush you have a handy and easy-to-use source of material for covering your foam. Take a dried flower head and split it into about six to twelve pieces, each bearing three or four florets and a short stem. The stems are wiry and can easily be inserted into the foam. There is no need to pack them tightly.

Sea lavender

Although sea lavender has been used to excess in many dried flower designs, judiciously used it can still play an important role in your designs as its densely flowered branches are an inexpensive and efficient means of covering foam. The stems lend themselves at the same time to creating an outline skeleton of the design.

Whatever the material you use, do not cover thickly or tightly as you may have a problem inserting your stem ends.

Plant material

You will probably have some idea of the plant material you want to use, even before you have selected your container. Before you go out and spend substantial amounts of money at a dried flower shop, assess what you have already in the home. It is amazing how much useful plant material can be gleaned even from a sad arrangement of sea lavender, helichrysums and grasses. Remove all plant material from this arrangement and sort into piles of the same type. Whatever the temptation do discard any that is faded and past its best. Sea lavender that may previously have dominated the display is well worth keeping to use with other flowers, perhaps on a less exuberant note. Take a sad 'silk' arrangement to pieces and add to different designs, perhaps storing some for a later occasion.

You can spray all the plant material you intend re-using with one of the proprietary products that will freshen them and remove the dust. Alternatively use a hair dryer very gently or carefully wash any 'silk' or glycerined material. Expensive plant material that has faded, such as peonies, can be sprayed with spray paint, or dipped in a flower dye.

Components

For a traditional medium-sized arrangement of flowers – for example, to fill a 20 cm (8 in) round basket or bowl – you will need at least four varieties of plant material in the colours of your choice, and probably more. This should include:

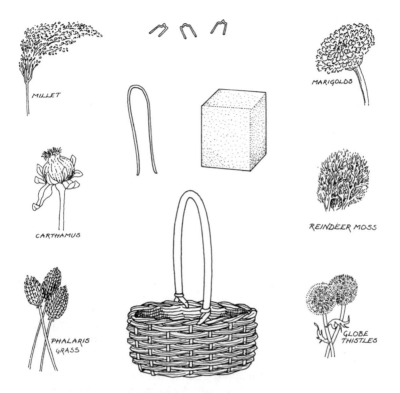

MILLET

MARIGOLDS

CARTHAMUS

REINDEER MOSS

PHALARIS GRASS

GLOBE THISTLES

- Branching material to create the shape. For example, approximately half a medium-sized bunch of millet, marjoram, oats or sea lavender. You could use sprays of artificial foliage, pressed beech or glycerined or dried eucalyptus.
- Focal material for contrast in shape and stronger interest. You will need approximately half to three-quarters of a bunch, for example, 14 marigolds, roses or helichrysums.
- Line material to link the branching and focal material and to give strength to the design; approximately half a bunch of, for example, carthamus, lavender or amaranthus.
- Filler material to complete. This can be anything of your choice. If your design needs a softer feel after the placing of the above three shapes add some more branching material. If you lack a smooth texture try adding poppy seedheads, globe thistles or grasses. In general, dried arrangements look better with more rather than less, but do leave some space between the flowering heads.

— 77 —

The basket in Figure 24 in the colour section uses millet for branching material, carthamus as line material and marigolds for focal material. Other material used to complete the basket are globe thistle and grasses.

Method

1 Place a sheet under your working area and perhaps a second one on the floor to catch the bits. Dried flower work can be incredibly messy!
2 Create the shape of your design with millet, eucalyptus or any branching material. With your first placement establish the height and use more of the same material, angled out of the side of the foam, over the rim of the container. Still using the same material fill the area between the central stem and the material angled over the rim of the container. As you do this remember two important keys to success:

   (i)   Ensure that every stem appears to radiate from one point in the centre of your foam whatever the shape or style of your container. This can only be achieved if the foam has been placed so that it is taller than the rim of the container.
   (ii) Remember the rules of good proportion. The material in your finished design should be one and a half times the volume of the container (see page 23). An easy way to achieve this is to place the central stem approximately the same height as the container, or marginally longer. As you angle material over the rim and sides of the container the proportions will automatically correct themselves.

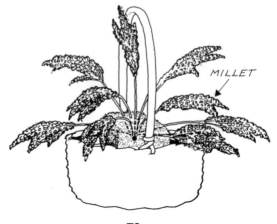

MILLET

3 Add some marigolds or other focal flowers. The shape has now been established so this material must be confined within the limits of the branching material. Place the focal flowers in the design at various angles to give greater interest. Insert the stems so that some flowering heads are slightly closer to the mossed foam than others so building up depth within the design and hiding some bare stems. This is called recessing the plant material.

MARIGOLDS

4 Add stems of carthamus or other line material through the design. Remember to place each stem so that it appears to have its point of origin deep in the foam.

CARTHAMUS

5   If you have not already used smooth textured material, add this now. At this point you may be thinking that your arrangement is awful. Do not worry. This is the point when most people despair. Persevere! Remember that dried flower arrangements need more material than their fresh counterparts.

6   Fill in your design with grasses, globe thistles or any other plant material until you are satisfied that it looks complete, yet still retains a little space. You will find that in the inner third of your design the material will be densely packed, less so in the intermediate third and it should have space in the outer third.

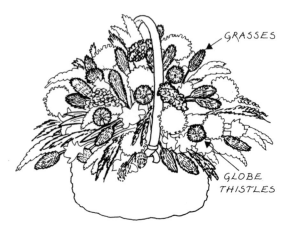

GRASSES

GLOBE THISTLES

7   Remember that each stem end must appear to originate from a point X. At this stage you may find it difficult to insert stems without them snapping as there will be little room for manœuvrability. This is when the stem(s), wired as described in Appendix 5, come into their own.

8

MODERN FLOWER DESIGNS

Dried plant material is particularly suitable for modern designs. The vertical, straight stems are frequently used as an exciting design feature. Other characteristics, as seen in Figures 7 and 18 in the colour sections, involve blocking plant material and placing stems so that each end has its individual point of origin. Each variety of plant material usually rises to a uniform height. For any modern design you will need the following:

——————— The container ———————

Suitable containers often have an angular form – for example, squared, rectangular or cylindrical – which harmonize with the straight lines of modern design.

Modern arrangements are often more sophisticated than their traditional counterparts. Unless the design is simply a tapestry, carpet or ground-work of plant material covering the base, baskets with handles are rarely suitable because the round shape of a handle detracts from the upward movement of the plant material. Suitable containers could be fruit and vegetable boxes, terracotta pots, gift boxes, wooden boxes or loaf tins.

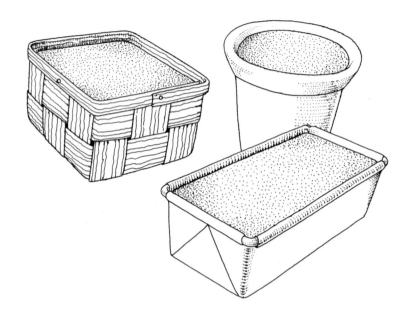

The foam

The size of the foam is important. It needs to be cut to fill the inside of the container completely but should stop just short of the rim. If your plant material has soft stems, use the foam intended for fresh plant material as its softer consistency will enable stems to be inserted more easily.

Material for covering the foam

If an abundance of plant material is used there may well be no foam to hide. If there is, moss is an ideal material. Alternatively, you can use dried leaves that have fallen from the stems of other plant material, such as roses, or pot pourri or even hay from the rabbit's hutch. It can simply be laid on the form, as the level is below that of the rim, or kept more securely in place with mossing pins or lengths of wire doubled into pins.

Plant material

In modern design great emphasis is placed on straight stems. Crooked stems can be used but they are usually placed well within the design so that they are hidden by the straighter stems or angled so that the head leans into the centre of the design. As mentioned in Chapter 1, it is focal and line material that is most often used to best effect in modern designs. Short, broken stems can be used in designs where no stems are evident.

Modern design that features vertical stems of a single variety

Method

1 For your first efforts try a design using only one variety of plant material, for instance 15–20 roses or about two bunches of lavender. Because the whole concept of modern design is based on straight lines, find a container such as a simple terracotta pot that has straight angular sides.

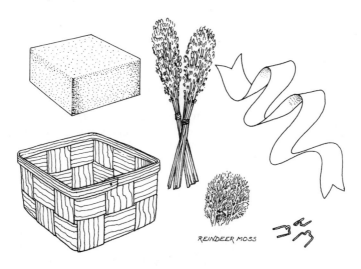

REINDEER MOSS

2   Establish the height limit of the design with a rose or a few stems of lavender placed centrally and cut the remaining plant material to the same height. If you have any crooked stems, place these around the central stem so they can be hidden later by the straighter stems. If you are uncertain as to how high to have your plant material, try about one and a half to two times the height or width of your container, whichever is the greater. If you have a visually heavy pot you will probably need to go for the taller of the two proportions. The tops of your plant material should all be on the same level. Gently turn small bunches of lavender upside down and bring all the heads to the same level in the palm of your hand. Cut and insert them so that the tips rise to the same height. This is more easily achieved if you arrange them at eye level rather than looking down at them.

3   Cover any visible foam with moss, dried leaves, small pebbles or short snippets of hydrangea. Tie a ribbon, or raffia, round the lavender, or round the pot to finish if so desired (see Figure 13 in the colour section).

Modern designs with more than one variety of plant material

Method

1   If you wish to progress to something more adventurous try using two or more types of plant material. If you have used lavender to create the height, add one or two rings of roses around the lavender at a lower level to give further interest. Alternatively, create height with wheat and surround this firstly with lavender so that the tips of lavender meet the bottoms of the heads of wheat. Then surround the lavender with roses.

2   You can now experiment with your plant material to create various blocks of colour, form and texture.

Try using sponge mushrooms, bun moss, cinnamon sticks, bundles of twigs and different varieties of plant material. It is important that the blocks of plant material should be well balanced. The skilful use of colour is therefore important, for instance you should not place ten

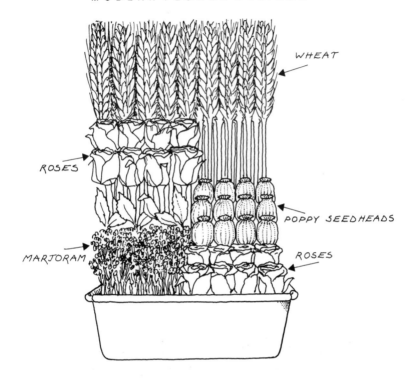

red roses to the extreme left of a design otherwise composed of neutral coloured wheat. This would cause the eye to veer to the left of the design and feel uncomfortable.

—— A modern groundwork design ——

Method

1   In a groundwork design, the container plays an important part and so should be carefully chosen to complement the plant material. It should be attractive but not powerfully dominant or you will lose the effect of the plant material, the lines of which could follow the shape of the container (see Figure 25 in colour section) or be placed in lines on the diagonal (see Figure 6 in colour section).

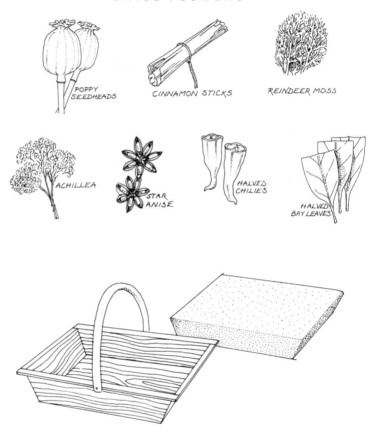

POPPY
SEEDHEADS

CINNAMON STICKS

REINDEER MOSS

ACHILLEA

STAR
ANISE

HALVED
CHILIES

HALVED
BAY LEAVES

2   You could use just one single type of flower or seedhead, but most of
your material needs to be focal, such as poppy seedheads, nigella,
achillea, hydrangea or roses. Branching material, such as marjoram,
tightly bunched together to give the appearance of focal material,
could also be used effectively. Many spices give good textural
interest, for example, halved chillies, short lengths of cinnamon
sticks or star anise. To give contrast of form try using fresh bay
leaves that have been halved and packed tightly into the foam so that
the even, cut ends are uppermost. They will dry in situ. Do not wait
until bay leaves are dry before you cut them as they would splinter
and fragment. These are used in Figure 18 in the colour section.

3   This type of design is best positioned so that it can be looked down
upon – perhaps on a coffee table or a low chest.

9

MODERN-
—— TRADITIONAL ——
FLOWER DESIGNS

As explained in Chapter 1 this style of arranging takes features from both
modern and traditional styles. It is a most attractive and easy style to
create. It does, however, use a lot of plant material – far more than you
may initially envisage. The aim behind the style is to juxtaposition
groupings of plant material carefully to give a display of colour, form and
texture.

The container

The ideal container needs to be symmetrical – a basket, a wash basin, a
pottery bowl, or a terracotta pot. It is easier to use if it does not have a
single handle or a spout. For your first efforts use containers that are
attractive but are not likely to overpower your plant material visually.
Natural plant material such as basketry always enhances plant material.

The foam

About two-thirds of the container needs to be filled with foam. If the cavity is filled completely it would restrict the natural flow of the plant material. The foam should rise slightly above the rim of the container, say 2.5 cm (1 in) for a small to medium arrangement. If your stems are not strong you could use brown 'Sahara' foam, or even the foam intended for fresh stems, but remember that the harder dry foam allows you more leeway when repositioning your stems as it is less likely to crumble, and it is also more suitable for heavier plant material such as 'exotica'. As the plant material is tightly positioned with little or no space between the focal heads, there is no need to cover the foam prior to placing stems.

Plant material

Because there is no space between the tips of the plant material ideally you need some material that has a broad, flat head to fill the area quickly, and without too much expense. Hydrangea, *Achillea filipendulina* and *Achillea millefolium* are ideal for this purpose. Branching material that can be tightly bound together to produce a flat mass of colour or texture, such as sweet marjoram, marjoram or linseed, is also suitable. The scale of the plant material is not that important because tiny flower-heads can be massed together to bring them into scale with, for example, one large head of achillea. It is focal material that is most important for success, for example, poppy seedheads, roses, nigella seedheads, hydrangeas. Do remember that you are going to need a lot of plant material and that strong stems are easier to arrange than weak ones.

Close colour harmonies are generally easier to work with. When using strong colour contrasts you must place them carefully in order to achieve good balance. Strong vivid colours will dominate, so if they are all on one side of the design it will be unbalanced.

Consider texture carefully as this, too, will distinguish between the blocks of plant material that you establish. At some point allow each grouping of plant material to abut plant material with a contrasting texture.

The modern-traditional design in Figure 3 in the colour section uses five varieties of plant material as described below. You will need:

Components

- A medium-sized rectangular basket about 22 cm (8.5 in) long. An oval or round basket could also be used.
- A piece of foam two-thirds the size of the cavity.
- Wire or a frog and fix to keep the foam in position.
- A quarter of a bunch of phalaris grass.
- Two hydrangea heads.
- Fourteen 'silk' roses. If you use dried roses you will probably need more than 20 as they are smaller.
- One bunch of poppy seedheads.
- About 20 heads of *Nigella orientalis*.

HYDRANGEA

ROSES

PHALARIS

NIGELLA ORIENTALIS

POPPY SEEDHEADS

Method

If your stems are strong you will probably not have to wire any but the last few.

1 Establish the highest point of your design. As a rule of thumb it should be the approximate height of the container once the stem end has been inserted in the foam. Unlike the upright modern design, where the height is approximately one and a half to two times that of the container, the modern-traditional design has plant material coming below the rim of the container. To maintain good proportion, therefore, the height is correspondingly less.

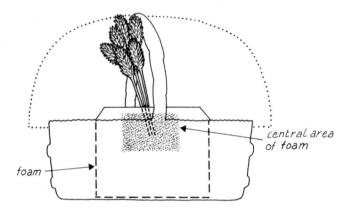

central area of foam

foam

Take one variety of plant material, for example, phalaris, and group it in several placements. Place the stems, one by one, into the foam so that there is no space between each flowering head. The secret of success is to position the stems so that they all appear to emerge not from a central point but from the central area of the foam. Your first placement of stems should not be bolt upright in the centre. The overall line of the finished design is a soft curve which is far easier to achieve if the first bunch is angled slightly away from the centre.

With this placement you have created part of the line of your curve. Every placement you make you must be conscious of creating another part of this smooth curved line so that the finished design has a softly domed shape, portraying a mass of colour, form and texture. The container is rather like a cottage loaf tin with the plant material creating the crust.

2   The balance of this style of design is symmetrical. This means that the plant material is weighted equally on either side of the central axis. You will not be creating a mirror image, as this would appear contrived. Balance is achieved through the careful placement of the different sized groupings of plant material and the judicious place-ment of colour. Any strong, vibrant colour that is distinctly different from the other colours in the design is going to be visually dominant. Therefore if this strong colour is placed in only one area the overall design may well appear unbalanced.

3   As a rough guide, in a small to medium sized design, make three separate groupings of each variety of plant material. Try to let every rough texture have a smooth textured plant material on at least one boundary and vice versa.

4   You have now established a general shape which can be filled in. If you now find it difficult to insert the stems you can either wrap stem tape firmly round them, close to the ends to keep them together, or use the wiring techniques explained in Appendix 5.

10

—— TOPIARY TREES ——

Topiary trees can be seen in varying shapes, styles and sizes. One of the most popular comprises a branch of a tree decorated at its apex with a sphere of plant material. More unusual designs consist of a cone shape, with or without a trunk, or a sculptured topiary tree with a swirl of moss, lichen, or perhaps the flat heads of achillea, wound round the tree trunk. If you understand the basic principles behind such trees you will soon be able to create one yourself and will also be able to adapt the ideas to suit your own personal tastes. The following instructions will inform you on how to create each of these.

—————— Topiary tree ——————

Components

Base

- outer decorative container – for the sake of good balance this should be approximately the size of the finished ball
- a plastic plant pot of a size that will fit inside the decorative container of your choice.
- plaster of Paris to keep your 'trunk' in place.

Figure 13 Topiary tree of roses, eucalyptus and lavender. Modern design of lavender and roses. Traditional design of sweet marjoram, phalaris grass, lagarus, statice, globe thistles and larkspur in a blue pottery bowl

Figure 14 Decorated basket

Figure 15 Modern-traditional design of exotics and marigolds

Figure 16 Topiary cones with a sculptured topiary tree

Figure 17 Modern-traditional design

Figure 18 Modern vertical design with freeze-dried roses and lavender

Figure 19 Topiary tree

Figure 20 Lavender, gypsophila, looped twigs and 'silk' daffodils

Figure 21 Wheat, chillies, hypericum seedheads, achillea, helichrysums

Figure 22 Blue and white 'silk' delphiniums

Figure 23 Mimosa, eucalyptus, roses, pomegranates, orange slices and glycerined oak

Figure 24 Traditional basket of flowers and foliage (see pages 78-80)

DRY FOAM SPHERE

PEBBLES

GLUE

WATER

PLASTIC POT

BRANCH

PLASTER

Cement or polyfilla can also be used but plaster of Paris is excellent. It is available from DIY shops or chemists and sets quickly. A minor disadvantage is that when water is added to plaster of Paris a chemical reaction takes place which generates heat. Therefore, if it is placed directly into a china container the heat may cause a breakage. You can, however, line your china or pottery container with foam and then pour the plaster of Paris into the protected container or alternatively if using a terracotta pot soak it in water for several minutes before use. A disadvantage is that if you do not use an inner container your topiary tree will be permanently fixed in a container you may later wish to use for another purpose.

Cement and polyfilla only set when they dry out so the process is a lot slower, and a good result not as certain, as the amount of water added has to be carefully gauged.

An alternative is to use plastic pots which may be purchased with a strong hard dry foam already inside. The trunk can be inserted directly into this foam, with or without a strong glue to give extra security. This is a quick and easy method but your tree will never be quite as secure as with plaster of Paris.

'Trunk' or stem

For your first efforts try to find a trunk about 25 cm (10 in) high. This will appear shorter when one end is embedded in the plaster of Paris and the other in the foam ball. The 'trunk' can be made from one of the following:

- a section from a wooden plait (see Figure 13 in the colour section)
- a bundle of long cinnamon sticks
- several twigs or lengths of bamboo garden pole cut to the required height
- a single thicker branch. A round ball supported by a single thin pole will look precarious and contrary to the laws of nature. You may need to sharpen the apex so that it does not destroy most of the sphere.
- for a larger tree, and indeed it can be as tall as a standard lamp, you can use a long thick tree branch or a broom pole. Try to avoid your ball looking as if it is on too spindly a support.

Sphere

Dry foam spheres are available in various sizes, but remember that the size can double once you have added your plant material. Alternatively, a block of dry foam can be shaped with a knife to form an approximate ball shape. If a large 'ball' is required you can take a square piece of 1.3 cm (0.5 in) gauge wire-netting, cut off the corners and place pieces of foam or tightly packed spagnum moss in the centre and wrap it to form a ball. If you are not using the more flexible green, plastic-coated netting you should use gardening gloves to protect your hands.

Plant material

This is discussed in detail in the designs below.

Method

1   If you are using a plastic garden pot, cover the base holes with wide sellotape or florists' tape to prevent the wet plaster of Paris oozing out. A few stones or a piece of lead can be placed in the bottom of the pot to give extra stability and reduce the amount of plaster of Paris that will be needed. Mix the plaster of Paris with water until you have a loose sticky paste, rather like pancake batter. Mix it with a stout stick which can be later thrown away. You will find that when you add water the plaster of Paris seems to shrink considerably in volume.

2   Place some of the mixture in the bottom of the pot and hold the trunk in place while you add more. If you are using twigs, rather than a single stem, bind them together at the top and bottom with strong tape. This will be later covered with plaster of Paris at one end and the sphere at the other end. Continue to hold the trunk until the plaster of Paris has set. Five minutes should be sufficient.

3   Impale your sphere very firmly on the 'trunk' to make a deep cavity. Remove the sphere and put sufficient glue in the cavity to hold it securely when replaced.

You are now ready to decorate your tree.

Design 1 – Using focal flowers

The easiest and quickest topiary trees to decorate are those where only one type of plant material is used. Rose heads, globe thistles, small cones, poppy seedheads, hydrangea, moss or nigella can simply be packed closely together to give one continuous block of colour and texture.

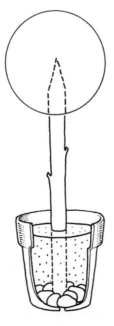

Bear in mind that the surface area of a sphere is much greater than you would imagine. Estimating the quantities needed is rather like guessing the number of sweets in a large jar! With roses you will need about 70 to cover a medium-sized ball although fewer roses will be needed if you lightly cover the ball first with reindeer moss. Nigella looks lovely and is not expensive. A tree can be created from one medium sized bunch. Hydrangea heads give a lovely effect and contrast can be given by adding a few poppy seedheads, helichrysums, cones or perhaps small golden mushrooms. When using more than one type of focal flower ensure that there is a contrast in texture.

If you have used spherical shaped plant material, such as globe thistles, you might find that however tightly you pack the material you still have gaps between the heads. You can fill these with individual flowers of statice or tiny poppy seedheads, both of which have sharp sturdy stems that can be easily slotted into small, awkward areas.

Topiary trees can be covered solely in flat moss or bun moss, the effect is stunning yet very simple. Use mossing pins or lengths of wire folded in two to keep the moss in place (see Appendix 5).

Design 2 – Using line material

A topiary tree using only line material can be most effective but the finished arrangement will be considerably larger than the size of the sphere. If you wish to use only line material for your first attempts try to keep to one variety. If you are using material that comes in more than one colour, such as larkspur, you could try mixing all the colours you have available. Cover the sphere in moss first if you are short of plant material.

When using neat plant material such as lavender, bunch three or four stems together to make them easier to insert into the sphere. Bunches that are too large will make it difficult to achieve a smooth, round shape, unless your tree is going to be correspondingly large. With lavender cut the stem to a sensible length so that on insertion only the flowering part is showing. With larkspur cut the flowering stem into at least two lengths, and perhaps more.

Start by making a placement vertically at the top of the sphere and then one at the bottom. Now make four placements round the circumference, equidistant from north and south. These four are important to the overall

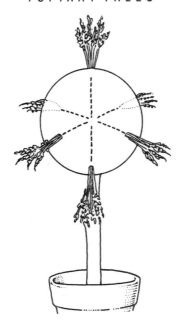

shape otherwise it could appear either slightly droopy or about to take flight. Each placement you make must appear to radiate from the central point inside the sphere.

Work regularly round the ball. If you are using line material such as lavender or larkspur you can trim the shape a little once all the pieces are in place and no one will be any the wiser. Plant material such as amaranthus will produce an enormous shape and any reduction in length should be made at the stem end as the bare tips will tell their tale.

Design 3 – Using line, focal and branching material

Unless you have plenty of plant material pin a certain amount of reindeer moss over the sphere before placing any plant material.

Create the ball shape with short lengths of line material as described in the method above for line material (see Figure 10.3). After you have created an outline of line material, add your focal material. Fill in with branching material but avoid using too many different varieties of plant material or the overall effect could be rather fussy.

Decorating the trunk

Once the tree is filled to your satisfaction you might wish to decorate the trunk. If so you could:

- attach ribbon tails just underneath the ball. If you use florists' polypropylene ribbon the tails can be curled with scissors or the blade of a knife.
- wrap ribbon round the stem in a spiral
- tie a raffia or ribbon bow around the stem
- plait some raffia and tie it round the stem.

Whichever method you use now is the time to put the tree and its plastic pot into a more attractive container. You could glue or simply place moss at the base of the tree to disguise the inner pot and give interest at the base. Alternatively you could shape a piece of foam to fit round the base of the trunk. This can be glued into place and decorated. Any elaborate decoration at the base should repeat at least some of the colours and plant material in the ball.

If you do not have a decorative pot you can glue moss or a palisade of twigs round the plastic pot and give extra security by tying raffia around.

Topiary cone

The cone-shaped base can be any of the following forms:

- dry foam sold in a conical shape.
- a block of dry foam cut into a conical shape.
- a block of wet foam cut into a conical shape.
- a piece of wire netting moulded into a cone shape and filled with pieces of dry foam or spagnum moss.

Although pre-formed conical shapes come in a limited range of heights they really are very easy to use. If you are using bulkier material, such as hydrangea, it is easier to retain a strong conical form if you use a larger rather than a smaller cone.

If you are going to cut a block of dry foam into a cone make sure that the sides slope sharply – again to ensure that, once decorated, the cone retains its shape. Begin by shaping one end of the block, that will become the base, into a circle. Make it the maximum size possible.

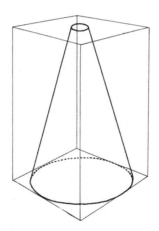

Create an apex about 1.5–2 cm (0.5–0.75 in) wide by slicing the sides of the foam block, at an angle, down to the base. Take your time and make lots of thin slices rather than a few chunky ones. You may think you need a narrower apex but be careful when you do this as you will need to insert plant material at the top. This is always rather tricky and if you have no depth of foam into which you can insert the stem ends it becomes extremely difficult.

If you want a very large cone use a wire netting shape filled with spagnum moss. Make a template of a square on newspaper. The height of your cone will be approximately the same as the side of the square. Cut the square diagonally in two. Place one of the triangular templates on to 1.3 cm (0.5 in) gauge wire-netting and cut. Fold the wire round to create the cone. Gardening gloves will protect your hands. Using wire cutters or suitable scissors shape the base so that it will stand. Pack this wire netting shape firmly with damp spagnum moss from which any twigs or debris should have been removed. Alternatively, you can use odd pieces of dried foam but it is more difficult to fill the entire shape.

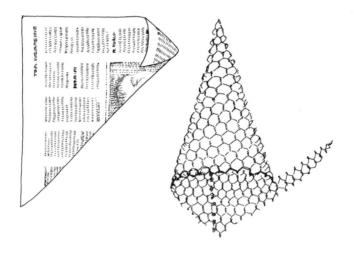

The cone can be placed directly on to a saucer or raised container. Alternatively, put a straight branch or pole in plaster of Paris, or a pot firmly packed with dry foam, and impale the cone on this. Since you will not need to have as much stem showing as for a topiary tree, the stem can afford to be quite slender without affecting the visual balance.

The cone can be decorated in various ways:

- Use snippets of hydrangea heads and decorate with focal material: roses, lotus seedheads, poppy seedheads, helichrysums.
- Use fresh box and finish with a spiral of focal flowers (see Figure 16 in the colour section).
- Cover with moss and decorate with flowers, leaves or seedheads (see Figure 16 in the colour section).

Fresh box cone tree

Components

- A block of wet foam. Using wet foam allows the box to dry out more slowly, thereby giving the leaves a smoother finish when dry.
- About three large bushy branches of fresh box.
- Twenty roses, fresh or dried.
- Plastic pot filled with plaster of Paris and a trunk.
- A rubber band.

Method

1 Gently carve the rectangular block of wet foam into a conical shape. As when making a dry foam cone the base should have the largest possible circumference within the obvious confines.

2 Soak the block for about two minutes, allowing it to sink under its own weight. It needs to be wet through, but not heavily saturated so, depending on the brand, you might need to leave it longer.

3 If you wish to impale your cone on a trunk, position a rubber band low down the trunk. This will prevent the cone sliding further down the trunk than you wish.

4 Condition the box by cutting it into short lengths and then placing these freshly cut ends into warm water for several hours in a cool place. Alternatively you could immerse the box for about an hour in warm water with a drop or two of liquid soap if the box is dirty.

5 Cut the box into small snippets about 2.5 cm (1 in) long and insert them, starting at the bottom of the cone. It is extremely important that the box is angled sharply upwards into the foam if you wish to retain a conical shape. The higher up the cone the sharper the angle will be.

6 Work steadily up the cone and carefully position the top pieces.

7 Create a spiral of roses round the cone, starting at the top. The roses can be fresh or dried. Fresh roses will be much larger at this stage but will shrink to about half this size when dried.

8 The fresh box and roses will dry in situ. All plant material shrinks as it dries naturally so make sure that you have packed your box tightly. However, you can add more later.

——— Sculptured topiary tree ———

Once you have your components together the design can be completed
easily and quickly. A taller tree, of say 60 cm (23 in) or more, is easier to
construct for your first efforts. The piece of wood in Figure 16 in the
colour section is about 75 cm (29 in) high.

Components

- A tall piece of wood. A length from a thick, straight branch works
  extremely well. If your branch has a curve it will be easier to use if the
  tip rises to a point in line with its base.
- A length of 1.3 cm (0.5 in) wire netting. The length needs to be about
  one-third longer than the piece of wood. Green plastic-coated wire
  netting will be easier to disguise.
- A large bag of spagnum moss. All twigs, etc, should be removed from
  the moss. It should be teased out and used damp but not wet.
- Flat moss. This can be acquired in bulk from specialist companies.
  Contact Robson Watley for details if you have trouble obtaining this.
  Alternatively, it can be scraped off damp drives, paths, low roofs, and
  from the lawn.
- A hammer and one or two medium-length nails.
- Lengths of wire, or mossing pins, for securing.
- A plastic plant pot.
- Plaster of Paris.
- An attractive outer container.

Method

1 Fix your branch in the plaster of Paris in the plastic pot so that it
   stands upright, using the method described on pages 94–5.
2 Cut the wire netting wide enough so that once rolled it will create a
   long sausage shape a little thicker than the tree trunk.
3 Make a short oval of tightly packed moss and lay it on one end of the
   wire netting.
4 Wrap the wire netting round the moss at this point and join the two
   sides together by threading the loose ends into each other. Flatten
   the end slightly so that you do not push this moss out of the wire
   netting when you add more. This is not as difficult as it sounds.

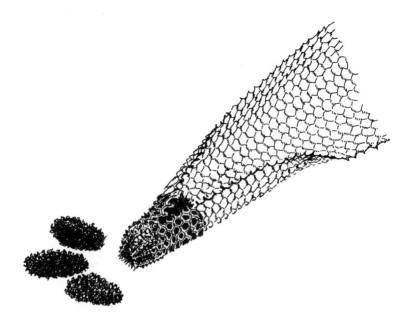

5   Create another oval of moss and push this down the enclosed section so that all the moss is tightly packed together. Bring another section of the wire over. Continue with this process until your long sausage is complete.

6   Wrap the long sausage in a spiral round the wood, with the tapered end at the top. You will find that it generally stays in place quite well. For extra security nail the sausage to the wood checking that it curves in the way you wish. You may not need to use more than one nail at the top to keep it in place.

7   Cover the sausage with flat moss or reindeer moss, or, perhaps, the flat heads of achillea. Use lengths of wire bent into hair pins or mossing pins to keep the moss in place.

If you do use flowering heads you will need rather a lot and it could make this sculptured tree very expensive to make. Flat moss can be torn into smaller areas to fit over the wire netting. When you have fixed your moss the spiral will be quite a bit thicker than your piece of wood. Avoid having the wood and the spiral of the same thickness – allow the spiral to dominate.

If you wish to make moss animals you would use the same method. Cut and mould pieces of wire netting to construct the head and body, then make the legs, paws and tail separately. These would then be filled with spagnum moss and wired to the main body before being covered with small sections of flat moss. For extra security you can wrap reel wire round and round the completed shape. Buttons and seeds can be used for eyes and noses, and slim stems for whiskers.

11

—— FLORAL RINGS ——

Floral rings, or wreaths as they are also known, are not only festive table decorations but attractive wall hangings – on their own or as part of a group of paintings – which can be displayed all the year round. There are shell rings, herb rings, moss rings, spice rings and many more. What they do have in common is a base. Some bases, such as a coathanger, are meant to be entirely covered, whereas others are meant to be featured as part of the overall design.

—— Bases designed to be hidden ——

Foam rings

Rings that are made from floral dry foam are light and easy to use but in order to look attractive all the surface area must be covered with dried or artificial plant material, ribbon or fabric. The rings are a neutral grey colour but spraying them green before you start will give a natural camouflage. Foam rings can be purchased in many sizes. The smaller ones can decorate the top or bottom of a candlestick (see Figure 25 in the colour section) or serve as a napkin ring, whereas larger rings can have candles added and be placed on the dining table. The dry foam rings which have been coated in a strengthening finish, manufactured by Hans J. Schwarzenburg, are very robust. All but the heaviest of plant material can be easily wired or glued on to these rings.

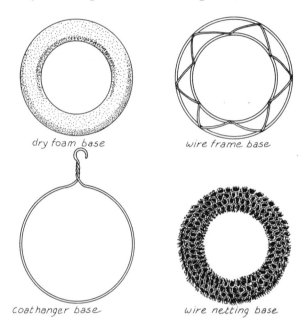

dry foam base

wire frame base

coathanger base

wire netting base

Wire netting filled with spagnum moss

The technique used is the same as that for making strong garlands and sculptured topiary trees (see Chapters 10 and 12). A piece of wire netting is cut the same length as the desired circle circumference, and about 20 cm (8 in) wide. Tease out some spagnum moss and remove any twigs or pieces of debris. Squeeze handfuls of moss into firm oval balls and place on the wire netting. The moss should be slightly damp but not wet. Roll one end of the wire netting over and join together with the protruding ends of wire. Push more compacted balls of moss into the opening and when it is packed tightly close the wire over to entrap it. Continue until you have a long sausage of moss-filled wire. If you feel at this point that the circle is going to be too thick and heavy, squeeze the wire netting to make it thinner.

Hook the two ends of the sausage together to form a circle and reinforce the join with pieces of wire or freezer bag ties. If you have stuffed your ring with firm, hard balls of moss it will be capable of supporting a great deal of weight. As the moss is moist it can also be used for fresh flower rings.

Wire frame covered with spagnum moss

Florists wire frames are available in a variety of sizes and styles. They are not expensive but if it proves difficult to find one, you can simply pull a wire coathanger out into a circle and use the hook to hang your ring. The overall finish will be little different. For your first attempt, a 25 cm (10 in) diameter wire ring works well. You need to pack firm oval balls of damp, freshly teased moss either side of the wire frame. Damp, rather than dry, spagnum moss is much easier to use. The moss is then kept in place with twine or reel wire, tightly wrapped round and round the ring at approximately 1.5 cm (0.5 in) intervals. Fresh plant material can also be used in this ring as the moss is moist. Some of the moss can be left exposed to be part of the design as the wire will be hidden in the moss if you have pulled the wire tightly.

Hiding the base

If you feel that you have to cover all the ring with flowers and seedheads you may wonder if the cost will be worth it. The secret is to cover the inner and outer extremities of the base with moss, statice or inexpensive plant material which you have in abundance and which is not visually dominant. You can also use hessian, ribbon or material round the ring. If you were to place focal flowers or brightly coloured plant material close to the outer extremities you would find that this prevents the eye moving smoothly and pleasantly round the design.

Using ribbon or material not only covers a lot of base quickly and easily (and inexpensively if you use material such as muslin or paper ribbon) but it also gives exciting colour and textural interest. Wired ribbon or a stiff length of fabric is ideal because it can be eased into a three-dimensional shape to give space and movement within the design. It should be pinned at intervals with mossing pins or short lengths of wire bent into hairpin shapes. The method below is for the floral ring shown in Figure 2 in the colour section, which is very easy to adapt to your colour scheme or to stock you have collected. Before you start you need to make a loop for hanging.

⎯⎯ **Floral ring on foam base** ⎯⎯

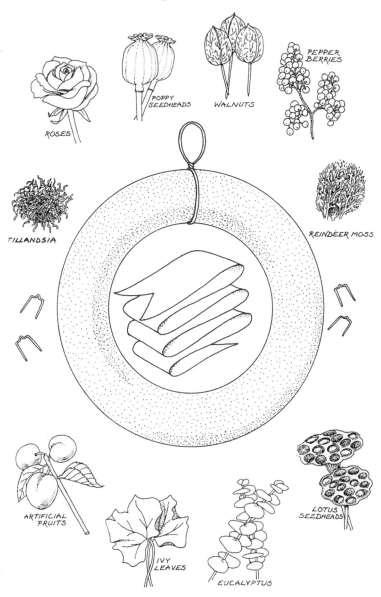

ROSES

POPPY SEEDHEADS

WALNUTS

PEPPER BERRIES

TILLANDSIA

REINDEER MOSS

ARTIFICIAL FRUITS

IVY LEAVES

EUCALYPTUS

LOTUS SEEDHEADS

Components

- Foam ring 25 cm (10 in) in diameter (you could use a larger or smaller ring if that is all you have available).
- Loop for hanging (wire, cord or ribbon) about 25 cm (10 in) long.
- Approximately 1.2 m (4 ft) of wide wired ribbon, about 5–7 cm (2–2.5 in) wide.
- Handful of green reindeer moss.
- Handful of white reindeer moss.
- Handful of green tillandsia moss. If you do not have this use more reindeer moss.
- One stem of large artificial fruit (try to find round fruit such as apples or plums rather than elongated or oval fruits such as pears or lemons). When purchasing be careful that your fruits are not more than twice the size of any other material you are using. In this particular design the walnuts are the transitional material, size-wise, between the fruits and the smaller plant material.
- Six red dried roses.
- Three to six walnuts, sprayed gold.
- Seven to ten medium-sized poppy seedheads sprayed gold.
- Sprigs of dried pepper berries (if these are not available you can substitute any berries, dried or artificial, or use more red roses).
- Eight to twelve mini lotus seedheads sprayed gold.
- Glycerined ivy, ivy seedheads and eucalyptus (a little dye has been added to the glycerine solution, see Chapter 5).
- Mossing pins or 8 cm (3 in) lengths of wire bent into hairpins – you will need a lot, far more than you would think possible. Start with about 50.

Method

1 With part of your length of ribbon, wire or cord make a loop of the required size for hanging on a nail. Tie the two loose ends tightly under the inner edge of the ring. This can be secured more firmly by pushing a mossing pin over the loop. If using a length of wire cover it first with stem tape.

2 Start at either the inner or outer extremity and secure the ribbon firmly with a mossing pin, or wire bent into a hairpin shape. Take the loose length of ribbon and position it in a loose uncontrived wave around the ring, pinning as you go. As it is the outer area of the ring

that is the most difficult to cover without spoiling the flowing rhythm of the ring, ensure that it is well covered. It is important to keep space and movement within the ribbon and for this reason it must not be pulled taught over the ring. Winding the ribbon round and round the ring is a waste of ribbon and actually restricts the movement. (Do not ladder the ribbon by pushing wires through. Pinch it at intervals and use the pins either side to secure.)

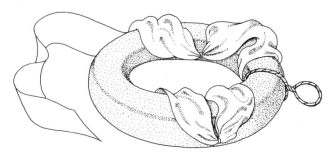

3 Cover areas of the ring with moss. Pay particular attention to the inner and outer areas.
4 Using good floral scissors or wirecutters take the fruits off the stem. Do not discard the leaves. Even if you do not use them in this floral ring you can use them in another design. Leave stems on the fruit sufficiently long that they can be firmly inserted into the foam base. As these fruits can be heavy it is prudent to add a dab of glue to the stem end after you have positioned all the fruits and are sure that they are placed to advantage. Place these at regular intervals round the ring. Ensure they are slightly angled inwards. If you place these even slightly outwards you will lose all the rhythm in the design.

5   Add the walnuts and poppy seedheads and then the roses so that they feature prominently. Push cocktail sticks through the soft spots of the walnuts and add a dab of glue to keep them in place. Fill in with your other material.

6   Use the remaining moss to cover any exposed foam. If you have any gaps just add any material you have available but remember to keep the majority of your components central or towards the inner edge, especially if they have either a large shape or a bright colour.

—— Bases designed to be exposed ——

Bases which are visually attractive in their own right are those constructed from plant material such as clematis, honeysuckle, vine, olive or ivy. Straw bases can be covered or be allowed to form part of the design.

Woody rings

These are easy to make simply by twining lengths of plant material round and round in a circle of the required diameter, tucking any loose ends into the ring when appropriate. The plant material can be soaked first in water to make it more pliable.

If you wish to purchase a woody ring decide on the right size for the position you wish to hang it and the right size for the amount of material you have available. Do not buy one that is too thin and weedy as you will find it more difficult to attach your plant material. Scale also plays a part. If you wish to use gourds, heavy fruits or large sea shells you will need a larger, more robust base than if you are using small flowers and seedheads.

Straw base

These can be constructed from sections of compacted straw held together with reel wire or twine. Ready-made versions can be purchased quite easily from garden centres and mail order companies. Straw bases are firm and robust and will therefore support heavy plant materials. It can be difficult to get wires through the hard packing of straw but material can easily be glued on with a glue gun.

Floral ring on vine base

This method describes how the floral ring shown in Figure 27 in the colour section can be made.

- A vine ring – this one is 30 cm (12 in) in diameter.
- Wire, narrow ribbon or cord for making a loop for hanging.
- A length of ribbon for a bow (optional).
- Three small compact heads of dried or silk hydrangea, plus some smaller pieces for filling in.
- Three silk zinnias (any round flower of a suitable size would work).
- Five roses (you could also use silk or paper roses).

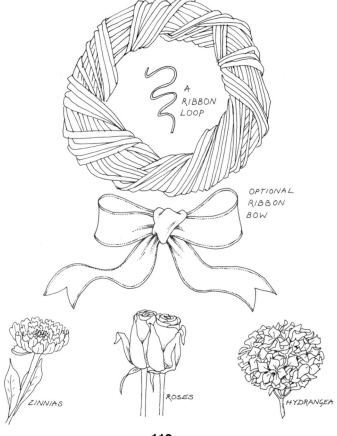

Method

1 Make the loop for hanging. This will be more exposed than for the foam base so use quality cord, ribbon or fabric. You could cover a long wire with stem tape to make it look less obtrusive. If using wire thread it through several of the twists of vine. Twist the ends together to form a large loop then move the join so that it is in the ring itself. Twist the wire at the top of the ring so that you have a neat loop which you can use for hanging.

2 Make a bow (see Chapter 5). Push a wire through the back of the bow so that it can be attached to the ring.

3 Decide where you want your hydrangeas. Three is a good number to use, but on a ring this size five would also look good. Place these and your bow in suitable positions. When you are satisfied with their placement cut the stems from the hydrangeas but remember to leave sufficient for the stem to be threaded through the ring. Secure the bow. If you wish to ensure that the material will stay firmly in place you can add a little glue to all the stem ends.

4 Add the other plant material. As with the foam ring remember the following:

(a) Any large or brightly coloured material should not be angled out of the ring.

(b) No material should be more than twice as large as any other component in the design.

5 Fill in with small pieces of dried or silk hydrangeas and/or roses so that the eye flows easily around the design.

12

SWAGS AND GARLANDS

Swags are wall decorations that are designed to hang without a visible background (look at Figure 34 in the colour section). If they are made on a flexible background two or more can be linked together to create a garland. There are several different bases suitable for swags.

Garlands can be defined as elongated, flexible decorations. They can be used for decorating staircases, fireplaces, door frames and tables. They look most effective when spiralled around posts and pillars.

Delicate garlands can be built up on ribbon. Stronger garlands can use soft rope as their base. Wire netting densely packed with spagnum moss is the ideal mechanic for bearing heavier material such as sprays of artificial fruit, large fir cones and filled terracotta pots. Whatever the mechanics used for garlands you will need a lot of plant material and a lot of patience but the results will be magnificent.

Swags

Bases

A piece of hardboard or pegboard

This should be cut to the required length and width. A suggested size would be 50 × 6 cm (19.5 × 2.5 in). It is important to remember that the finished item will be slightly longer and quite a bit wider, once you have covered up the base. See if your supplier can make a hole for hanging near the top end of the hardboard. Pegboard already has holes, but be sure the hole you wish to use for hanging is centrally placed.

Cut about five rectangles of foam not larger than 7 × 4 × 2.5 cm (3 × 1.5 × 1 in). You would have to use a lot more plant material to cover them if they were larger and you would have less movement in your design. These need to be fixed securely down the centre of the base lengthwise, following the shape of the base, leaving a gap of 2–3 cm (1–1.5 in) between each piece. Ideally use a glue gun for its strong adhesive qualities or a special glue for use with dry foam – there is one made by Oasis – which will bond the wood to the foam securely.

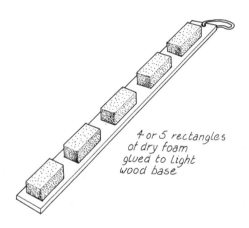

4 or 5 rectangles of dry foam glued to light wood base

A moss-filled length of wire netting

The technique is similar to that of a wire netting floral ring filled with spagnum moss, referred to on page 106. You will need a length of 1.3 cm (0.5 in) gauge wire netting that is slightly shorter than the required length of the finished swag. Green plastic coated wire netting is more easily disguised than the grey galvanised wire netting and if you are short of material, or simply like the effect of the moss, you can leave areas of the swag uncovered so that the mechanics become part of the design. The netting needs to be about 15 cm (6 in) wide in order to produce a firm roll with a width of about 5 cm (2 in) wide. Remember that if you fully cover all of the mechanics the overall effect will be wider and longer.

Fresh spagnum moss should be teased out and compact handfuls should be placed at one end of the wire netting but squeeze it first to remove any excess water. At this point the two sides should be brought together over the moss and the loose ends of the netting interwoven to fasten them together securely. Flatten this filled end slightly so that the moss stays in position as you stuff more moss firmly and tightly into position. The shape can be adjusted once you have completed the sausage. Continue until you have filled the length of wire netting. More moss should be pushed down to make it really firm. Continue working along the wire netting, packing the moss as tightly as possible and encasing it as you go. Flatten the back so that it will lie flat.

To avoid scratching or damaging a wall, fabric or sections of black binliner can be glued or pinned on to the back of the swag for protection. To give extra support the sausage of moss can be fixed to a base of hardboard or pegboard. Long nails can be hammered through the base and into the wire netting which will help to support the sausage.

A straw plait

Straw plaits are readily available at garden centres throughout the country and, of course, from specialist shops. They are inexpensive and easy to use. The simplest method is to glue the plant material directly on to the plait. Alternatively stems can be wired and the wire threaded through the plait. It is difficult to insert dried flower stems directly into the straw plait. If you want a longer swag you can wire and glue two plaits together.

STRAW PLAIT

The components listed below are for the swag in Figure 34 in the colour section, the base of which was constructed from hardboard and rectangles of foam.

It is not essential to include exactly the same items. For example, any dried seedheads can replace the lotus seedheads, artificial flowers can be substituted for the pomegranate and dried peonies could replace the silk peonies. If you do not have some of the stated material use more poppy seedheads, cones or whatever you have to hand. A ruling by the Department of Trade and Industry (DTI) now prohibits the sale of realistic small berries and fruits unless they are so securely attached to a backing that it would take a major force to dislodge them, so you should always beware of using these, especially if there are small children in your household.

Components

- A piece of hardboard approximately 50 × 6 cm (19 × 3 in).
- Five rectangles of foam approximately 7 × 4 cm × 2.5 (3 × 1.5 × 1 in).
- Wire, twine or cord for hanging.
- White and green reindeer moss.
- One spray of artificial burgundy plums (these are often available in large department stores, kitchen and gift shops).
- One spray of burgundy peonies or any other large round flowers. They could be silk or dried.
- Ten cinnamon sticks.
- Gold thread to bind cinnamon sticks together in twos.
- Red roses.
- Three pomegranates.
- Five cones.
- Six lotus seedheads.
- Five to seven walnuts.
- Seven to ten poppy seedheads.
- Five coconut roses.
  (The swag in Figure 34 in the colour section shows some of the above five items sprayed gold. If you wish to have this swag on display all the year round you might prefer not to spray them.)
- One spray of small red berries.
- Two to four stems of artificial, dried or glycerined foliage.

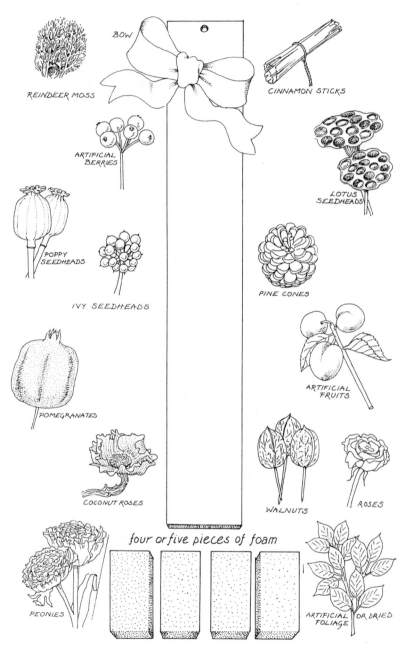

REINDEER MOSS

BOW

CINNAMON STICKS

ARTIFICIAL
BERRIES

LOTUS
SEEDHEADS

POPPY
SEEDHEADS

IVY SEEDHEADS

PINE CONES

POMEGRANATES

ARTIFICIAL
FRUITS

COCONUT ROSES

WALNUTS

ROSES

PEONIES

four or five pieces of foam

ARTIFICIAL OR DRIED
FOLIAGE

- Three stems of ivy seedheads (those used have been glycerined).
- Wide bow for decorating the top of the swag.

This is the basic list for a completed swag of approximately 56 cm (1 ft 10 in) but if you need a little more material to make it even more generous and full, add whatever you have available that would be in keeping with the harmony of the swag.

Method

1   Make a loop for hanging the swag. If it will not be hidden by the bow, cover the wire with stem tape or create a more decorative hanging.
2   Cut the flowers off the peony stem. If your stem bears three flowers in different stages of development place the bud, or smallest flower, high up the swag but not right at the top. Place the largest flower just below half way down and the third flower towards the bottom. If you place them at various angles you will create more interest, but the most important middle flower should be placed more or less centrally. When you are sure of their positions you can insert the short stem ends, adding a spot of glue if so wished to give extra security. Avoid packing a large, solid shape at the very bottom of a swag, as it will look as if it is about to fall out, or at the extreme top, where it will look top heavy.
3   Glue wood picks, or lengths of heavy gauge wire, to the pomegranates and firmly insert them into the foam. Pomegranates look lovely in a swag and should be shown to full advantage.
4   Make five bunches of two cinnamon sticks each. Wrap wire round to secure them together leaving ends that can be inserted into the foam. You can decorate the wire by wrapping gold thread over it and round the cinnamon sticks (raffia or jute twine could also be used). Secure if necessary with a little glue. Place these at intervals to create a swathe through the swag, making sure that the five placements look visually balanced.
5   Cut up the spray of red berries and add them in groups where colour is most needed. Glue in very firmly, thinking of the DTI!
6   Add the coconut roses. The roses are the parts that were once attached to the base of coconuts. If you are unable to find them, add any dried seedhead that gives interesting texture. If the thick stems of the coconut roses are difficult to insert sharpen them or cut off the whole stem and add a false one made of wire or part of a wooden stick.

7 Add the red roses and the other items.

8 The background must be entirely hidden. This can be achieved by using reindeer moss, artificial leaves and perhaps small pieces of hydrangea, if you have these available.

9 Add a bow to the top of the swag, covering most or all of the hanging loop. Details of how to make a bow are given in Chapter 5.

The table centrepiece in Figure 30 in the colour section was created in the same way, using berries, fruits, and mini terracotta pots which were filled with mixed beans from a health food shop. A wire was passed through the hole in the base of the pot, taken over the rim then twisted at the base. Alternatively you can glue a piece of wire to the side of the pot but this is not as secure. The long-awned wheat was bunched in pairs and placed at various angles through the design in a similar way to the cinnamon sticks in the swag described above.

Garlands

As previously mentioned, garlands use more material than you might originally consider and they take a considerable amount of time to prepare. They also have a propensity for turning to show a bare rear just when they are not supposed to, so fix them firmly into position. Despite all these disadvantages they create an atmosphere hard to equal. The garland should be hung in position before it is completed so that you can cover any exposed areas that appear once it is hanging.

There are many ways to create a garland but perhaps the three easiest methods are the following:

Wire netting and moss garland

The method for this is exactly the same as for the swag, floral ring or sculptured topiary tree. Your completed garland will be heavy but will be capable of supporting a great deal of plant material. It is ideal for decorating churches, large buildings and fireplaces, particularly at Christmas when fresh long-lasting evergreen foliage can be added to give bulk to the garland.

If you wish to taper the ends this can easily be done by squeezing the wire netting ends together. Use green plastic-coated netting if you wish to expose the moss as part of the design. Use several lengths of mossed wire, to make the length you require, and then join them firmly together with wire.

Rope or ribbon garland

Wired bunches of flowers can be wired on to a length of robe or ribbon to give a light and delicate garland suitable for decorating a table or staircase. You will need a soft rope or ribbon of the requisite length and bunches of dried or silk material to be bunched and wired on. The technique is similar to that for the bridal headdress, described in Chapter 14. The rope or ribbon is decorative in itself and you may, for the sake of economy or effect, only decorate it at intervals.

To make a stronger garland a stout rope can be covered with spagnum moss. Compacted handfuls of moss should be firmly bound on to the rope with reel wire or strong garden twine. Bunches of plant material are then wired on. The wires should be pushed through the mossed rope and the ends then turned back into the moss. The moss can be part of the design. If you use natural green twine or garden reel wire it will be easily hidden by the moss.

Simply Garlands

Simply Garlands is the trademark of a company that produces green plastic foam holders which can be linked together simply to form a garland or a swag. Rectangles of foam are placed in these holders, or cages, and then decorated. The holders can also be used to create floral rings and swags.

Whatever basic materials you choose be warned that you will need a great deal of plant material and a great deal of patience. With the wire netting or 'Simply Garlands' cages you can cover a lot of mechanics first with hydrangea or statice. You can, in fact, use any material that has a firm strong stem and will cover quickly and relatively inexpensively. Most artificial flowers also cover mechanics efficiently but this can be costly.

13

FLOWERS IN A VASE

A successful arrangement of dried flowers in a vase, without foam to keep the stems in place, can be quite difficult to achieve because the stems are naturally stiff and rigid and have no leaves to soften the design. If, however, you arrange dried flowers with silk, glycerined or paper plant material there are advantages to be gained.

Silk foliage and flowers have wired flexible stems that can be angled and bent within the arrangement to give movement, and over the rim to link the flowers and the vase. Dried flowers contribute a natural form, colour and texture and often give a wonderful fragrance to the room. Glycerined foliage can provide an additional softness and flexibility to the design. Desiccated flowers give intensity of colour and trueness of form while twigs, branches and cones add to the originality and excitement of the design. If you are using parchment or paper flowers the colour can be changed with watercolours and a fine paint brush. Just use as if you were painting a picture, but remember to spray these flowers with fire-resistant spray if using near candlelight. Full details on how to use a desiccant are in Appendix 3.

The vase or container

The vase here means any container that is taller than it is wide. When choosing your vase consider the following:

- In traditional design the stems of dried and silk flowers are the least attractive part of the design. Consequently, if you place them in a clear glass container, it is best to add marbles, pot pourri, shells, glass nuggets, pebbles or even fabric to hide them. Another way to disguise the stems without losing the delicate quality of the glass would be to use a cut-glass vase rather than plain glass. Cut-glass vases never go out of fashion. They have an ethereal quality that is ideal for flowers such as freesia, yet the intricacy of the cut helps to hide the stems.
- Vases that have a very strong pattern or a shiny texture will overpower most flowers. White containers are very dominant, particularly if they are shiny as well. However, white flowers in a white vase with perhaps the addition of green or cream-variegated foliage, or pastel flowers, can give a stunning effect. If you are using a patterned vase, pick out one or two colours and use different tints, tones and shades of these colours for an unfussy effect.
- If you like the shape and size of the vase but the colours do not complement the surroundings take a piece of fabric – perhaps a plain piece, or even a patterned one which matches the room – and stand the vase on the fabric. Lift the fabric so that it totally covers the vase, then tie it near the top with cord, braid, ribbon or raffia, remembering to tuck in the ragged edges.
- The heavier the container the more material you will need to get the proportions right. If a pottery or stoneware vase is shaped then it has a lighter visual effect.

Plant material

1   A lot of silk foliage is very realistic but do check that the back spines are not too dominant as they will shine through obtrusively when you put the arrangement in direct light. Bend the leaves so that the spines are not so obvious. Small-leaved varieties, such as box, are always a safe bet, as are those with a plain dark green colour.

Leaves with serrated edges can be more realistic than those with a smooth leaf margin. Variegated silk foliage can make a design look very busy. It is best used with material that is simple and not too colourful. Silk foliage that has leaves going round the stem, such as eucalyptus, or leaves that branch off at many angles, is easier to use than stems with flat branches and leaves all facing the same direction.

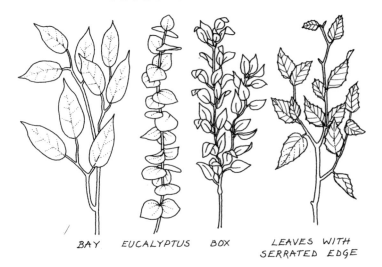

BAY   EUCALYPTUS   BOX   LEAVES WITH
SERRATED EDGE

2   If you are using silk flowers play with each stem before arranging. Pull out the leaves from the stem into natural positions. Bend, rather than cut the stems. You can always cut them later if you are sure you would like a permanent display.

3   A single variety of flower with foliage is often successful. Rather than buying all the flowers in exactly the same colour try to buy those which are close to each other on the colour wheel, or are tints, tones and shades of the same colour. Silk flowers imitate natural flowers and if you buy a fresh or dried bunch you will notice the varying colours in each flower.

4   If you buy a few large flowers, say three, you will usually be able to manipulate the size by opening or closing the petals. Have each one in a different stage of development, on different lengths of stem (see Figure 28 in the colour section. Strips of clear cellotape can be placed in a criss-cross over the opening of the vase to provide support for a few stems.

5   Bear grass is a tough long grass-like foliage that can be purchased fresh from many florists and mixed with dried or silk flowers as it lasts for weeks even without water. It can be treated with glycerine and dye to last indefinitely. An artificial silk variety is also available. To be effective, all the grass should be bunched together in a rubber band and allowed to explode, rather like a fountain. If you buy silk bear grass, the individual sprays are usually attached to one length of stem. Bunch three or four sprays together with an elastic band.

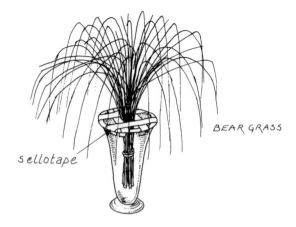

BEAR GRASS

sellotape

6   Colour can also compensate for lack of volume. Vivid or dark colours appear to weigh more than pastel colours. Fewer vivid or dark flowers will be needed to offset the weight of the container than those of pastel colouring.

7   Flowers generally look their most effective if the harsh line of the rim of their container or vase is softened by the downward flow of the plant material. This can be achieved by:

- using the artificial flowers and foliage so that their wired stems can easily be angled to bend over the rim of the container.
- using glycerined foliage which retains its flexibility and can 'fall' over the rim.
- using long-lasting fresh foliage such as bear grass, branches of long-lasting twisted willow, or camellia, which will last for weeks once cut. If you wish to add water to an arrangement containing fresh, dried and artificial material you can dip your artificial and glycerined stem ends in clear nail varnish or wax to prevent them getting soggy.

8   Massed flowers of one type in a vase always look good, but there must be enough of them. One bunch of freesias without help can look lost. Adding some foliage gives bulk.

9   The plant material should be about one and half to two times the height of the vase for good proportion. Alternatively, if the plant material is not tall enough, the volume of the flowers used can compensate for the lack of height. Therefore less height means more flowers.

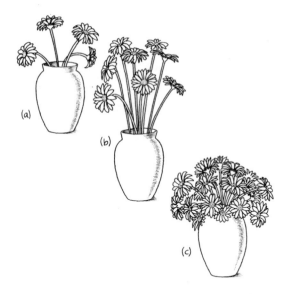

The volume of flowers used should be about one half to two times the volume of the mass of the container. Conversely you can compensate for having only a few stems by increasing the height.
10 With a mixture of artificial and dried flowers it is easy to follow the seasons. There is no need totally to replace all the plant material. Roses can be mixed with tulips in the spring, larkspur in the summer, hydrangeas in the autumn and pine at Christmas. Do not mix flowers that obviously belong to different seasons, e.g. daffodils and chrysanthemums or poinsettias and delphiniums. With the fear of sounding obvious, avoid having daffodils on display in autumn.

Fragrance

One easy way of giving a fragrance to your flowers is to put pot pourri in the vase. Ideally, try to use a pot pourri that contains the flowers you have in the design, e.g. a rose pot pourri, a lavender pot pourri. If that is not possible, try to use an autumnal mix in an autumn design, perhaps a pine pot pourri at Christmas time, a hyacinth or lily-of-the-valley in the springtime and rose and lavender in the summer.

Floral atomisers have been specially developed for dry and silk flowers. They are available in a wide variety of fragrances and can be sprayed directly on to the flowers. If you match the flowers with the fragrance, the effect can be quite stunning.

It is now easy to buy flower oil essence complete with dropper. Choose oils that are not alcohol based as these are likely to stain the flower, whether it is dried or silk. For best results squeeze a drop right into the centre of your flower.

14

– WEDDING FLOWERS –

Creating fresh flower bouquets and headdresses that will stand up to the exertions of the wedding day is a skill that is usually best left in the hands of professional florists. Creating long-lasting wedding flowers is possible for untrained hands as they can be prepared in advance, thus taking away the urgency.

This chapter will advise you how to create an informal bunch of flowers that, when tied with co-ordinating ribbon, will give a long-lasting floral memory of the occasion. There is also a method for making a bridal or bridesmaid's headdress. This takes time to make as there is a great deal of wiring and stem-taping involved, and patience is required. A bridesmaid's floral ball is easy to create with dried or silk flowers. A simple buttonhole is also described.

The colours used in Figure 32 in the colour section are appropriate for a winter wedding. Use different flowers and different colours to suit the time of year.

If the bridal bouquet is fresh and the bride wishes to keep it as a permanent memento she can preserve the flowers with a desiccant and reassemble it under glass. Full details are given on page 138.

———— Bridal spray bouquet ————

One of the simplest forms of bridal flowers is the bouquet of dried or silk flowers assembled into an uncontrived shape and finished with a sumptuous bow. A bouquet is usually larger than a posy and is flat at the back so that it can lie over the arm. Be careful if you want to use glycerined material as it can sometimes ooze glycerine, especially if kept in a damp atmosphere. It will need to be treated with a clear sealing product such as Super Surface Sealer produced by Oasis.

This shape of bouquet looks lovely as a wall decoration and can be hung on a picture hook to give pleasure throughout the year.

For a dried bouquet, avoid choosing flowering stems that are thick in relation to the amount of flower or leaf, or your design will become bulky. If you cut any stem ends make sure that they are sealed in stem tape, if unsightly. The flowers can be softened by the addition of fresh, dried or glycerined eucalyptus or long-lasting bear grass. The following components are for the bouquet in Figure 32 in the colour section.

Components

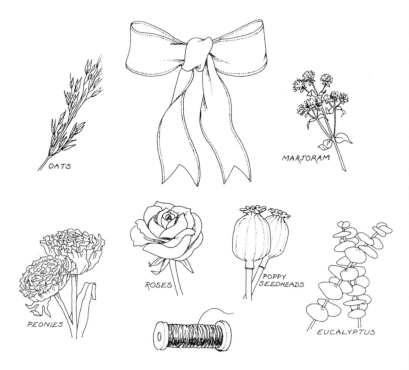

OATS

MARJORAM

PEONIES

ROSES

POPPY SEEDHEADS

EUCALYPTUS

- One bunch of oats to lie at the back. You could also use grasses or linseed. They need to have long stems and a green or a soft colouring or lightly pressed to frame the other plant material. For an autumn wedding, glycerined brown oak or beech foliage could be used. Whatever outline material you choose, it should have interest partly down the stem and be sealed if glycerine has been used.
- Eighteen to twenty roses, you could substitute any focal material according to taste.
- One bunch of marjoram. If you do not have marjoram any fine branching material will work, e.g. *Alchemilla mollis*, gysophila.
- Five peonies sprayed gold – this is optional but has been introduced to create a link with the gold used in the bridesmaid's floral ball and the bridal headdress.
- Twelve poppy seedheads, sprayed gold – again, this is optional.
- A few sprays of eucalyptus – again this is optional but has been introduced to link with the eucalyptus in the bridesmaid's ball and the headdress. This has been sprayed with Super Surface Sealer for protection as it has been glycerined and dyed.
- Reel wire or twine.
- Wired ribbon bow. Paper ribbon could also be used.

Method

1   Lay the oats in a kite shape so that the stems cross low down. Leave a few stems to add at a later point. You will need to bring interest down to this point so do not cross the stems too low down if you are short of plant material. Take the reel wire or twine and wrap it round the stems several times. If you are only planning to hang the flower spray on the wall it is not as important to make every stem as secure. You could therefore keep the oats in position at this point with an elastic band, while you place the other plant material on top.

2   Layer some of the roses and about half of the marjoram and eucalyptus on top of the oats, keeping within the outline you have created, thereby allowing the oats to frame the other flowers. Position the top roses quite high up, about 5 cm (2 in) lower than the tips of the oats. Mix the plant material together to obtain an informal bouquet of flowers. The stem ends will probably be shorter than those of the oats but this does not matter. If they do not come down as far as the crossing point move the elastic band further up the stems

or wrap a few more lengths of reel wire or twine around the bunch, bringing in the newly added stems.

3   Add the peonies lower down the design and use the rest of the roses, marjoram and eucalyptus so that they create a link through the design, wrapping them in with the reel wire or twine when you feel the need. Bring the plant material down to the point where the stems cross and use it to hide them.

4   When you feel that the bouquet is sufficiently full make a few final wraps with the reel wire or twine.

5   Add the ribbon bow to cover the wire. If you have quality ribbon you can make a simple half-knot or use one of the methods described below.

6   If there is a gap which might need the addition of an extra rose, tuck this in where appropriate. You could put a dab of glue on the stem end to ensure it stays in place.

7   Trim all the stem ends, either straight across or in a 'V' shape.

8   Add your bow. As an alternative to using the florists' ribbon you could also create a bow made from the same fabric as the bride's dress. Details of how to make bows is described in Chapter 5.

Bridal headdress

When creating a bridal headdress you need to make sure that it fits the bride correctly and feels comfortable. The headdress in Figure 32 in the colour section is suitable for either a bride or bridesmaid. You will need:

Components

- Four 30 cm- (12 in) long medium-gauge wires.
- Stem tape to cover the wires.
- Reel wire.
- Half a bunch of oats.
- One bunch of red spray roses.
- About 12 gilded mini poppy seedheads.
- One third of a bunch of marjoram.

MINI POPPY SEEDHEADS

SPRAY ROSES

MARJORAM

OATS

You can substitute any suitable material but always keep scale in mind. Gypsophila or *Alchemilla mollis* would also look pretty in this headdress.

Method

1 Hold two wires in the left hand and two in the right. Let them overlap by about 5 cm (2 in), hold in one hand and then strongly bind them together into one continuous length, first with reel wire and then with stem tape.

2 Create an 'eye' at one end by forcing a small amount of wire back on to itself.

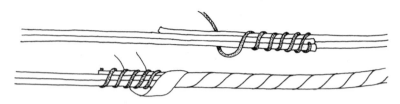

3 Find a large rounded jar or vase and bend your length of wire round it to create a smooth, loose curve. Now place the wire ring on the bride's or bridesmaid's head and ease it to the correct shape and size. Cut off any excess wire leaving sufficient wire to make a hook which can be attached through the 'eye'.

4 Choose a mix of plant material, enough to make about 15 small bunches. Each bunch should have approximately the same amount of material so that volume and weight is distributed equally throughout. Cut the stems quite short and wire each bunch. This is necessary because it is important that on such a special day flowers do not fall out at an inappropriate moment. If you find that the stems are brittle and collapse when you wire try stem taping prior to wiring to give them more strength. The stems of each bunch should then be covered with stem tape to hide the wire. You may find that for the small flowers it is easier to use the stem tape if it is split in two. Refer to Appendix 5 for the wiring technique.

5 Start at the eye and attach the first bunch with stem tape so that flowers cover the 'eye'.

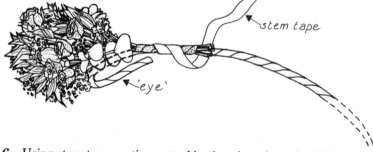

stem tape

'eye'

6 Using stem tape continue attaching bunches along the full length of the wire. Let each bunch overlap the previous one, and place one bunch slightly to the left and then one slightly to the right to get a full, rounded shape. Work in one direction only for this particular head-dress. Place the headdress on the bride's head after you have worked about one-third of the way round to check that the flowers have been

positioned at the correct angle for maximum effect and that it is full enough.

7   If you are making more than one headdress, be sure to label each so that they fit the right head on the day.

———— Bridesmaid's floral ball ————

This floral ball in Figure 32 in the colour section is simple to make.

Components

- A dry foam sphere – not too large as you will increase the size with your plant material.
- A length of ribbon which, when doubled over, will create a suitable length for carrying, probably about 25 cm (10 in).
- A long heavy-gauge wire, sufficiently long to pass through the diameter of the ball when doubled.
- A skewer or knitting needle – this can be impaled on the ball to make the decoration easier.
- Glue.
- Half a bunch of spray roses.
- Twenty to thirty mini poppy seedheads sprayed gold.
- About three stems of marjoram.
- About two stems of dried or glycerined eucalyptus.
- A handful of reindeer moss.

Method

1   Bend the wire in two to mark the central point and then wrap this around the ends of your piece of ribbon so it is firmly attached.

2   Bring the two wire ends tightly together and push them through the ball so that they protrude from the other side with the ends as close to each other as possible. You might not get them straight through to the other side on your first attempt but keep on trying. It does not matter if the ends are slightly uneven. Turn the protruding ends back into the ball. You may wish to add a dab of glue at the point where the ribbon ends and the wire meet the top of the ball.

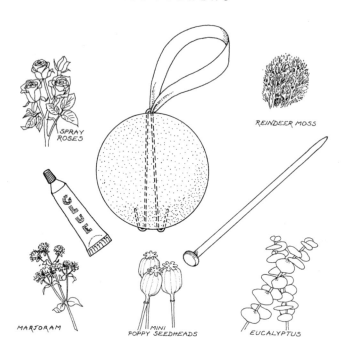

SPRAY ROSES

REINDEER MOSS

MARJORAM

MINI POPPY SEEDHEADS

EUCALYPTUS

3   To decorate the ball you can first cover it with a little reindeer moss.
4   The procedure now is the same as for the head of a topiary tree. For this particular ball insert short pieces of eucalyptus at intervals. Then add the roses and poppy seedheads on short stems. Finally, insert short sprays of marjoram to fill out and complete the ball. As you fill the ball you might find that handling damages the plant material, therefore impaling the ball on a skewer or needle may make your insertions easier.
5   If so desired, take a further length of ribbon and make a few loops. Attach it to a wire and insert this at the bottom of the ball.

Buttonhole

Now that you have tried wiring and using stem tape you will find that a small buttonhole hardly warrants explanation. However, one method of producing a buttonhole is the following:

Components

- Light rose wire.
- Stem tape.
- One or two stems of oats or other green plant material.
- Two or three roses depending on size.
- One stem of marjoram.
- Two or three poppy seedheads sprayed gold.

Method

1 Cut the oats into three short lengths. Arrange these on a flat surface to form a kite shape with the stems crossing low down.
2 Place the other plant material within the shape created by the background material.
3 Wire the stems together and cover with stem tape.
4 Attach a safety pin, or a pin used for making jewellery, through the back of the stem tape.

5 Thin ribbon can be used to decorate the stem, ending perhaps in a neat bow.

A fresh flower bouquet
preserved with desiccant

If you wish to preserve a fresh flower bridal bouquet with desiccant the procedure is given in Appendix 4. The following information will also help you.

It is important that the flowers and foliage are preserved as soon as possible after the event. If, however, some of the flowers have wilted – which is quite possible – they should be revived, prior to preserving, by cutting the ends and placing them in tepid water for several hours. If they cannot be placed in a desiccant immediately after the wedding, then place them in a cool dry place overnight. You will need at least five kilos of desiccant to preserve an average-sized bouquet. This is one of the reasons why it is so important that you experiment before the event so that you will be able to gauge just how much you will need for the size of bouquet you wish to preserve.

As the different flowers and foliage in the bouquet will not need the same length of time in the desiccant it is strongly advised that you dismantle the bouquet first. (A small buttonhole need not be dismantled. It can simply be placed in the desiccant.) Before you do this take a close-up photograph. You may think that you will always remember every detail, but a couple of weeks later when your flowers are preserved and ready to reassemble, you will be glad that you took the photograph for reference.

If possible ask the bride to request minimal wiring in her bouquet. Holes in the petals, made by wires, can be obvious when the plant material has dried. Even if there is no wiring some of the flowers in the bouquet will be damaged, so you could ask the florist to supply you with some extra flowers and foliage. You will find, however, that you will probably not use all the flowers in the bouquet.

For speed the flowers can be prepared in desiccant in the microwave. Do remember that every single wire must be taken out before preserving this way. If you are not using a microwave, just cut the wires short, about 2.5 cm (1 in) should suffice. Alternatively, if the flowers have not been wired, do leave them a short stem.

As it is so important that your flowers are preserved correctly it is advisable to practise before the event, particularly if you are using a microwave. Ideally, but not essentially, have several containers ready so that each can take a different type of flower.

Remember to take care when adding the desiccant over the flower-heads. Do not pour desiccant directly over the heads, as this could damage them. Gently nudge the desiccant between the bottom petals first, perhaps using a paint brush.

Before assembling the flowers make sure that they are completely free from moisture. It would be awful to have your design complete and behind glass and to find that several of the flowers become stained by moisture. Ensure that all the particles of desiccant have been removed. Do this with a fine paint brush or the tip of a cocktail stick. Give the flowers a light spray of acrylic sealant which can be purchased from most art shops and from the companies that sell desiccants. Hair spray seals the surface of the flower, but tends to yellow it.

While the flowers are being preserved find a suitable picture frame or have one made. An ordinary picture frame is not suitable. Your frame needs to have a recess of at least 7.5 cm (3 in) so that the flowers will not be squashed up against the glass. Most picture framers will willingly make these up for you.

The backing fabric that you use could be the same material as the wedding dress. It should be tightly stretched and glued at the back of the frame, not the front, as however carefully you use glue it will usually show through fabric.

Use a clear glue to fix your plant material. Play around with the various flowers and foliage to make a good design or to follow the design of the original bouquet. Place some flowers in position first and build up layers of flowers. You could also add lace, ribbon or pearls from the wedding dress. Do check that the glass will not crush any of the flowers before you glue the plant material into position.

When the design is to your satisfaction and each flower and leaf is glued into position turn the picture over and tap gently to see if any petals fall. These can then be glued into position before you seal the frame. Give the completed design a light spray of sealant. Make sure that the inside of the glass is clean and seal the design. The completed design should be hung out of direct sunlight.

Flower bouquets can also be preserved by pressing. Details on how to create a pressed flower picture are given in Chapter 15. The process for a wedding bouquet is the same but do try simpler pictures first.

15

SEASONAL GIFTS
AND DECORATIONS

Any of the designs described in previous chapters can be given as gifts. Yellow, blue and white can be introduced for Easter festivals. A profusion of colours is associated with high summer whereas autumnal and harvest colours are brown, orange and yellow. To give a special Christmas feel some of the plant material can be sprayed gold and mixed with reds and green. The addition of candles always give that special atmosphere.

It is easy to make original inexpensive gifts from a few flowers and a little bit of know-how. The following ideas are for those who would like to make items for Christmas bazaars, gifts for teachers, or to give a token of appreciation to a neighbour or friend.

– Pomanders or clove-studded fruits –

Clove-studded fruits as well as the more elaborate pomanders were used as long ago as Tudor times to ward off unpleasant odours. Cardinal Wolsey used to carry a clove-studded orange, while poorer people scented the domestic apple. The scent of cloves is supposed to keep moths away and prevents clothes from smelling musty. To make a fruit pomander which is a lovely gift, and one which children will enjoy making, you will need the following:

Components

- Prime cloves – ideally with well-formed heads and strong stems
- Thin-skinned fruit – thicker skins can be pierced first with a needle or bradawl. Small Seville oranges or organic oranges work well. Lemons and limes offer a contrasting shape. Ensure that your fruit is fresh and of good quality.
- Sellotape or florists' tape to outline the areas where ribbon will be later added. The ribbon is not put on at this point as it might get marked.
- Half an ounce of orrisroot – this is a white powder available from health food shops. Orrisroot, derived from the root of the Iris germanica, is a fragrant fixative. This means that the scent of the orrisroot does not diminish with time and makes the fragrance of other spices last longer.
- Half an ounce of mixed ground spices such as cinnamon, cloves, nutmeg.
- About 1.1 m (3 ft 7 in) of narrow ribbon.
- A paper bag.

Method

1 If you wish to hang your pomander rather than simply place it in a bowl wrap the tape round the fruit to divide it into two or four neat, equal sections. The ribbon must be the same width as the space you are leaving. Pack the cloves into the uncovered area, leaving a little space between each clove as the fruit will shrink as it dries. If you have difficulty inserting the cloves use a skewer or bradawl first to make a hole.

2 Remove the tape from the fruit. If a lot of juice has flowed from the fruit dip it in cold water and dab on kitchen towel. If you do not do this the juice will adhere to the orrisroot and spices which can become lumpy.

3 Mix equal amounts of orrisroot with the other mixed spices. Besides being fragrant the brown colouring of the mixed spices will disguise the colour of the white orrisroot which can stick to the fruit even when it has dried out.

4 Put the fruit in the paper bag and ensure it is covered by the orrisroot and spices. Leave the fruit for about six weeks in a dry place such as

an airing cupboard or a high shelf. When the fruit has dried it will have lost weight.

5 Now add the ribbon. Wrap it round the fruit and glue it into position. Create a loop at one end of the ribbon and glue it to the top of the pomander. Add extra loops if so desired.

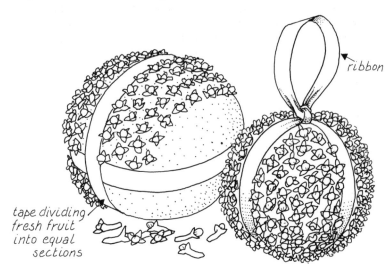

ribbon

tape dividing fresh fruit into equal sections

fruit shrinks when dried

Pot pourri

With the move away from aerosols, pot pourri has become extremely popular over the past decade. Pot pourri should be fragrant and visually attractive. It can be simple or complicated to make. Whether you buy the basic pot pourri or create it from flowers in the garden you need to keep it out of direct sunlight as this will quickly bleach out the colour. If you are placing the pot pourri in a large room you will need a larger quantity than if for a small room. If the room is warm the fragrance will dissipate more quickly than in a cooler room, but do avoid long-term dampness as this could cause mildew to form.

What you need is a floral base which gives bulk and to which you add the other ingredients. Ideally it should be fragrant but this is not essential. A floral base can be created by one of the following methods:

Floral bases

- The easiest floral base is a ready prepared variety which you can personalise by adding extra ingredients. Chemists, department stores, garden centres and gift shops all sell pot pourri. Choose one that you find personally attractive, both visually and aromatically. In 'designer' pot pourris many items, such as wood shavings, flowers and leaves, may have been dyed in order to intensify the overall colour theme. The traditional mixes of rose and lavender and garden flowers are always popular but there are now many combinations that are bolder and have wonderful textural interest. These may include golden mushrooms, bark, lotus seedheads, cinnamon sticks, lichen moss, pine cones or cedar roses. Many of these more exotic combinations have a more 'masculine' aroma, based on the fragrances of various aftershaves. Pot pourri is often presented for sale in sacks and is sold by weight. It is also sold in pre-packed bags. It is advisable to buy the latter as the heavier items, such as some seedpods and cinnamon sticks, tend to sink to the bottom of the sack and the lighter components, such as fir cones rise to the surface. In the pre-packed bags you know you will get a good balance of ingredients.

- When you arrange dried flowers you will accumulate lots of fallen flower-heads. This is inevitable, but not disastrous, for you can put all these flowers to good use. Instead of throwing them away gather them together and keep in a bowl or bag until you have a certain quantity. They do not have to be fragrant because fragrance can be added at a later point in the form of revitalising oils which can be added to any absorbent ingredient.

- The most time-consuming base is probably the most satisfying and long lasting. It is composed of petals and fragrant leaves from the garden. So that their colour and fragrance is intense they should be picked at the peak of their perfection. These petals are going to be dried so do not pick them after rain or a heavy dew, but do pick them before the sun is at its height as this causes their fragrance to dissipate into the atmosphere. If possible pick for fragrance, for example, old-fashioned roses, stocks, Daphne, mock orange and hyacinth, mint, rosemary, lemon verbena, geranium leaves. Spread the petals and leaves on absorbent paper in a dry airy room on a cooling tray or in the sun. Turn them occasionally until they are completely dry.

Additional material

Spices, dried citrus peel, herbs and fragrant woods

These are ingredients that do not necessarily give bulk but give added fragrance. There is a myriad of dried material that you can use. Spices from the kitchen cupboard – anise, cinnamon, cardamom, nutmeg, allspice, ginger – can all be added according to taste. Citrus fruits can be thinly pared and the skin added in order to sharpen and freshen the aroma. Fragrant woods or wood fruits, perhaps ready impregnated with sweet smelling oils, can be added.

Fixative

Fixitives have traditionally been added to pot pourri mixtures to help retain fragrance. They combine with the natural fragrance produced by the plant and make it less volatile. Orrisroot powder is probably the most easily found fixative. Other fixitives, such as musk and ambergis, have been used in the past but as these are animal based search out orrisroot or calamus powder, from the sweet flag, or coumarin powder obtained from plants such as woodruff, meadow sweet and melilot. If you add your fixitive to a fragrant pot pourri and keep them together in a sealed bag for a few weeks, the natural fragrance will last much longer.

With the advent of synthetically produced revitalising oils a fixitive is not an essential ingredient of pot pourri. In fact most commercial producers of pot pourri no longer use a natural fixitive. But a natural fixitive will lessen the need for regular additives of fragrant oil and might well prove less expensive in the long run.

Add approximately 25 grams of orrisroot powder to every litre of base and additional material. If you are using another plant-based fixitive you will need to add approximately double the amount.

Revitalising oils

Both essential and synthetic oils are available for adding to pot pourri. Essential oils are the natural organic substances which give plants their aroma. As they are only present in small quantities they are more expensive than synthetic oils. Many synthetic oils now smell amazingly true to nature and are available in a multitude of fragrances from shops throughout the country. Do choose an aroma that links with the visual appearance of your pot pourri. Avoid adding an exotic fragrance to a cottage garden mixture. Because of their strength it is no longer essential to use basic ingredients that have a natural fragrance. You can instead concentrate on colour and texture. Follow the instructions on the bottle or add two to six drops of oil to every litre, depending on the strength of the oil.

Preservative

All pot pourri mixtures need to be kept dry. If there is any danger of damp place a small sachet of salt, borax, silica gel or Flower Dry under your pot pourri.

When you have the colour, form and texture of your pot pourri to your satisfaction place it in bowls or dishes where you wish the fragrance to linger. If you have used a fixitive remember to mix this with the ingredients in a closed bag for several weeks before exposure to air.

However faded or old your basic pot pourri there is no need to throw it away. You may remove it from view but can continue to add revitalising oils. Place the pot pourri in organza bags and insert them between your clothes or hang them up in the wardrobe. You can place pot pourri within a section of an old pair of tights and tie the end round to the clothes rail in your wardrobe. If you cover the pot pourri with thick fabric the fragrance will not be able to permeate through.

—————— Decorated basket ——————

Decorating a basket is a novel way to present a gift of pot pourri, chocolates, Easter eggs, pomanders or perhaps scented wooden fruits. It is an ideal opportunity to use up left over plant material with short broken stems. If, however, you are using long-stemmed plant material you may be surprised at just how much material you will need to cover even a small basket. Look at Figures 5 and 14 in the colour section. The first thing you will need is a basket with a reasonably wide rim. Flowers can be bunched and wired on to the basket, or glued straight on. Perhaps the easiest and most effective method is to cut rectangles of foam and glue these directly on to the rim of the basket. These pieces of foam need to be as small and thin as possible but substantial enough so that the stems can be securely inserted.

Chamfer the pieces of foam and cut off the corners so that the foam more or less follows the contours of the basket. The pieces of foam do not have to nudge each other. Leave a little space between the pieces.

On a medium to large basket it is a good idea to use ribbon or fabric to help cover the foam and to add texture, colour and form. Pin this into position in the same way as when fixing fabric on floral rings. You can pin a little moss on to the foam so that you do not have as much surface area to cover with plant material. On a small basket, moss and snippets of hydrangea cover foam quickly and efficiently.

You can now add your flowers. Do remember scale. Individual stems of lavender added to the decorated basket shown in Figure 14 in the colour section, would be completely out of scale with the rest of the plant material. Other points to remember is that any large shape should not be on the outside of the design. The eye should follow smoothly round the shape of the basket rim and therefore heavy shapes should be placed upright or slightly inwards. Angle your plant material to give interest and ensure that you have textural contrast. You need smooth texture to enliven the other plant material you have used. If the basket is large and your plant material is heavy use a glue gun to put glue on the stem tip so that it stays firmly in place.

———————— Fragrant gift boxes ————————

Any empty paper, material or wooden box can be transformed into a sweet-smelling gift with only a few flowers, a short piece of ribbon and perhaps a few ingredients from the kitchen cupboard.

Components

- A small empty box.
- A piece of thin cardboard, perhaps from a cereal box, slightly smaller than the base of the box, but repeating the same shape – a square, a circle, a rectangle. This can be covered in a scrap of material. At this point check that it fits tightly inside the box.
- A small piece of foam, a few centimetres deep for a small box, cut to the same size as the cardboard.
- Approximately 12 cm (4.5 in) of ribbon (for a small box) to create a loop.
- A piece of the same ribbon to wrap round the sides of the foam (optional).
- Plant material or spices to cover your foam. The focal plant material used needs to be in scale with each other.

Method

1   Make a loop with the ribbon and glue the ends to the centre of the foam. Alternatively, wrap wire round the ribbon ends, insert the wire ends through the centre of the foam and then turn them back into the foam (this is the same procedure as when making a floral ball).
2   Glue the foam to the cardboard.
3   If wished glue ribbon round the sides of the foam.
4   Place the plant material or spices geometrically in lines or in circles.
5   Place the decorated cardboard into the box and add a few drops of fragrant oil to intensify the fragrance of the material you have used. Revitalising oil can be added when needed.

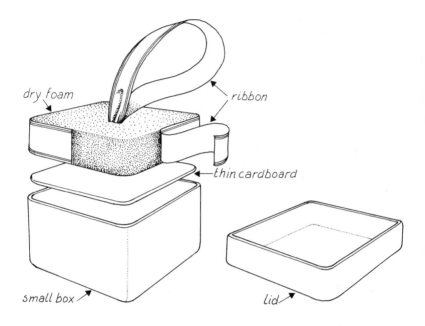

dry foam

ribbon

thin cardboard

small box

lid

Wall baskets

An example of a sweet-smelling herb wall basket, with a wide pouch or pocket, can be seen in Figure 17. It is important that you follow the shape of the basket when placing your plant material so that you have longer plant material in the centre and shorter at the two sides.

Flat baskets with a small pocket are even easier to make, cost very little and brighten up a wall very effectively. You need to insert enough foam into the basket's opening so that it covers about half of the opening area and rises a little bit above the level of the opening. This will enable you to have a downward flow of plant material. These baskets really do not need a lot of plant material to look effective. The foam can be partially hidden with a little moss, or snippets of hydrangea, before placing any stems. You can fill the pouch with foam and create a 'mini garden design' with upright stems. Whatever the design do make sure that it is well balanced. Do not heavily decorate one side unless you balance the other side, perhaps by putting a paper ribbon bow on the handle.

Decorative twig bundles

This is very simple to make. Bunch together a number of twigs to form a bundle. Any twigs would be suitable but dogwood and some varieties of willow have wonderful coloured bark which gives added interest. Alternatively, you could use cinnamon sticks. Twist a wire round the stems to keep them in place. Wrap some decorative ribbon round the wire and decorate with a few flowers.

Christmas tree

The photograph in Figure 33 in the colour section shows a delightfully decorated Christmas tree. It is almost as easy to make three as one, so why not make one for yourself and the other two as gifts or charity contributions.

Components

• Picture hanging wire

- A piece of fibre board, thin plywood or hardboard cut to the shape below. Cardboard will also work if it has a heavy enough density. The sides of the equilateral triangle in the photograph are 30 cm (11.5 in) long.
- Dark green spray paint.
- UHU glue or a glue gun.
- A selection of dried plant material sprayed gold and no more than 5 cm (2 in) in length. Suggestions would be walnut shell halves, beech masts, alder cones, acorns and acorn cups, wheat ears, various sized poppy seedheads, small fir cones, larch cones, sycamore wings and dried aquilegia and *Magnolia grandiflora* seedheads, helichrysums, almonds and cob nuts.
- Plant material to define the shape of the inner triangle. These can be slightly longer than 5 cm (2 in) in length. Perpetual sweet pea pods are ideal as they curl when dry. You could also use ears of wheat or twirls of pasta.

Method

1 Make a hole at the top of the tree for hanging, then thread the picture framing wire or very strong thread through the hole.
2 Spray the shape green and, when dry, mark a triangle within the shape, about 3 cm (1.25 in) from the edge, with pencil.
3 Glue the long sweet pea pods, pasta or wheat, over this line to form the inner triangle.
4 Fill in the rest of the triangle by gluing on nuts and seedheads, starting from the bottom. Try to get a good mix of form and texture.

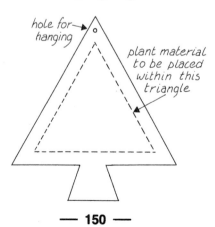

hole for hanging

plant material to be placed within this triangle

Pressed flower cards

It is probably prudent to start using your pressed flowers in a very simple way. The results are so effective that it will give you the confidence to progress from a simple flower card to a landscape picture, where petals and leaves are skilfully cut and shaped to create the actual background which becomes part of the design (see Figure 35 in the colour section).

To get the feel of making pressed flower cards you can start by folding a sheet of deckle-edged or plain, heavy-quality notepaper. If you are pleased with the results you can go on to use a special craft card. Whether you use notepaper or special cards you will need to cover your work with a thin adhesive film, or have the cards laminated for protection. The easily acquired adhesive film is perfectly adequate for your first or even second efforts. This, and the special craft cards, may be purchased from art and craft shops or mail order companies. Specialist laminating companies would be happy to laminate your efforts. Their addresses can be found in the Yellow Pages.

Place your card on an uncluttered surface along with your collection of dried plant material. You will also need a glue that dries clear or is clear, a PVA glue is ideal. Tweezers are ideal for moving the plant material around the card.

The following information, which will help you create a good design, is also applicable for more ambitious work.

Design points

1   As a general rule it is better not to mix flowers of overtly different seasons, e.g. snowdrops and roses.
2   Avoid using too much plant material or too many different varieties.
3   If you have a plain background leave a good margin round your design. Only fill about two thirds of the available area and leave one third blank to give space which will enhance your design. If you are creating a crescent leave one third open. If you have a short crescent add perhaps a butterfly made of plant material or a few flowers in an appropriate position to give good balance. Leave a little more space at the top than the bottom.

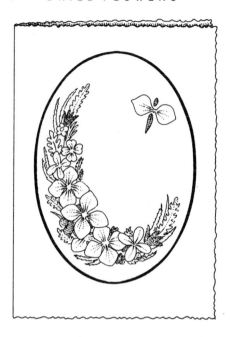

4 Avoid straight lines unless you are creating a 'botanical' picture. Curved stems are generally more useful.

5 Do not heavily overlap plant material. This will only detract from the colours as well as subdue them.

6 It is easier to design within an oval than a rectangle. If you have a rectangular card, make an oval template and use this to draw an inner oval shape as in Figure 36 in the colour section.

7 Avoid placing large single flowers, such as a large pansy, in a design otherwise composed of tiny flowers and leaves unless they are linked by plant material that is transitional in size.

Method

1 Place assorted material on the card and play about with the plant material to create the desired shape using tweezers. Keep out of a draught so your design remains still.

2 Use a glue that will dry clear or is clear. This is a time when a hot glue gun is not appropriate. Use one of the PVA glues.

3 Put some glue on the tip of a cocktail stick or darning needle and dab a

little of it onto the back of your flowers and leaves. Try to glue where there is a double thickness.

4   Once the design has been glued into position give the glue a little time to dry before placing your sheet of special adhesive film over the picture. Put this on very carefully. Only peel off the top few centimetres of film. Check that it is straight before removing the remainder of the film. At this point you will be extremely glad you used glue, otherwise the flowers would respond to static and lift themselves off the backing and on to the film.

——— Pressed flower pictures ———

The process of creating a picture rather than a card is very similar. The only difference is in the technicalities.

Components

●   A picture frame with hardboard backing and glass – both must be a tight fit as it is important that moisture does not get into the picture. Make a suitable allowance if you wish to cover the backing with fabric rather than having a card mount. Glue the fabric at the back, not the front. Non-reflecting glass does as it implies but it does tend to deaden the effect.

●   A soft thin piece of foam positioned between the fabric and the backing to give a soft yet professional look to the design. Because the foam is spongy it allows the heavier material to sink in further, giving a more even finished surface to your design.

Method

1   Design your picture on the card or fabric mount and use a fine paint brush to remove any small bits that may have fallen on to the picture.
2   Clean the glass inside and out.
3   Assemble the picture ensuring that the plant material makes contact with the glass.
4   Hang the picture out of direct sunlight as the flowers will fade much more rapidly.

Decorated candles

This is deceptively easy to do. You will need an iron, a spoon with a thick rounded handle, a few dried flowers and leaves, and a candle. It is perhaps easiest to start with a thick cream candle.

Heat the iron and when it is hot place the back of the spoon against the iron and allow it to warm. Start by placing a single flower or leaf on the candle – not too high up – and rub the back of the spoon over the wax and flower. A little of the wax melts and covers part of the pressed flower so keeping it in place. Following this method, add flowers and leaves according to taste. You will need very little plant material to get an exciting yet professional effect.

Decorated hats

Not only are decorated hats suitable for wearing to a special event, they look most attractive hanging on a wall all year round. The head cavity can be filled with pot pourri and encased by a piece of gauze sewn across the back. This will allow the fragrance, which can be revitalized with essential oils, to fill the room.

A hat in a neutral colour gives plenty of scope for decoration. You need to decide whether you wish to decorate with plant material all the way round, or simply at the back or side. You must then decide if you wish to glue the plant material directly on to the hat or whether to glue it first to a ribbon band. If the hat is inexpensive the former is probably wise as this method is very simple and secure. The advantage of using a decorated ribbon is that it can be removed if the flowers fade or if you wish to change the colours, but do make sure that the plant material you use is not too heavy. A ribbon band should not be too wide or it will sag or pleat. Having measured the length of ribbon required, make an allowance for about a 5 cm (2 in) overlap. Lie the ribbon flat and glue on your plant material. The ribbon can then be lightly sewn on to the hat. Bows at the back always look attractive.

If you wish to glue directly on to the hat, make sure that you have worked out your design first.

—————— APPENDIX 1 ——————

—— Preserving by hang drying ——

Hanging flowers upside-down is the simplest method of preserving flowers and seedheads successfully. Most flowers can be dried by this method, even small-trumpet narcissi. However, flowers whose petals encapsulate space as an integral part of their form, such as tulips and lilies, lose much of their charm when dried by this method. Foliage generally becomes too brittle to be of use. A more suitable method for foliage involves glycerine, which can be found at most chemists, and water. This method is described in Appendix 2. Fresh, well-conditioned eucalyptus leaves do dry well, however, and aspidistra leaves turn an interesting brown and take on lovely curves. Both eucalyptus and aspidistra leaves do not become too brittle to use in arrangements.

Hang drying plant material is attractive in itself and can add a decorative feature to your house. Much advice can be given to perfect this technique but basically the key to successful drying is speed. The quicker the drying process the better the colour will be. So how can this be done?

Method

1 Choose your drying time carefully. A hot dry summer spell is ideal. A damp November is not.
2 Plant material should be picked when it is dry. Do not pick flowers when the dew is still on the ground, or after a rain shower. If you have no alternative but to pick flowers with moisture still on the flower-head, place them in a vase with their stem ends in water until the flower-heads are dry. Just to complicate timing even further, avoid picking in the mid-day heat as the flowers may wilt before you are in a position to dry them. Process as soon as you have picked them. If you are drying for scent, pick just before the sun is full out as it breaks up the flowers' fragrant chemicals.

3 For dry air to penetrate to the centre of your flowers there needs to be maximum air movement, not only between the flowers as they hang, but in the room in which they are hanging.

The flowers should be tied in small quantities. Most of the foliage should be removed and the flower-heads slightly staggered. Put only a few flowers together – the amount will vary according to the size of the flower-head. As a rough guide about 30 stems of lavender, five roses or one spike of delphinium.

Commercial flowers refresh the air in the drying room continuously by means of heaters and ventilators which suck the moist air away. For the individual an attic can provide the perfect answer as the air is being constantly recharged under the eaves and through the tiles. This is one instance where loft insulation does not pay! Not everyone has access to an attic but there are other solutions:

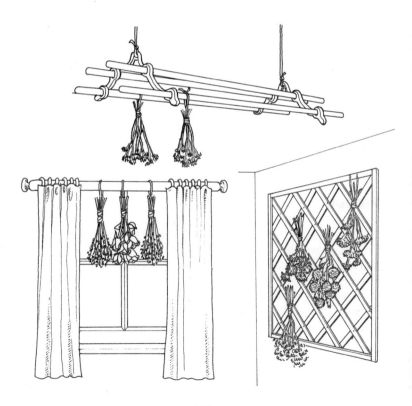

Figure 25 Decorated ring for a candlestick with a shade. Modern groundwork design in square bark container

Figure 26 Decorated straw hat

Figure 27 Twisted olive ring (see page 112)

Figure 28 Three white parchment peonies

Figure 29 Wall basket of dried peonies, galex leaves, helichrysums and beetroot slices with 'silk' alstroemeria

Figure 30 Wheat, terracotta pots, blackberries, mushrooms, seedheads

Figure 31 Advent ring of fruit, berries, moss, dried flowers and glycerined ivy leaves

Figure 32 Flowers for a winter wedding

Figure 33 Christmas tree with garland

Figure 34 Christmas swag (see pages 117-120)

Figure 35 Pressed landscape pictures

Figure 36 Pressed flower card

- The airing cupboard, but prop the door ajar for the damp air to escape.
- Basements, but only if they are damp-proof.
- Curtain rails in rooms where curtains do not have to be drawn. Avoid too much direct sunlight as this causes rapid colour fading.
- A garage or shed as long as it is during a hot dry spell and the flowers are removed once dried.
- Trellis work, attached to the wall or ceiling of a kitchen or utility room.
- Lazy Susan clothes dryer.
- Kitchen hanging rails with hooks for mugs or kitchen accessories. Put the mugs in a cupboard and use the hooks to hang your flowers.
- Fit an extendable curtain pole into a window and suspend your flowers.

There are many more ideas and places. The enthusiast will find them.

4   Tie the stems together tightly as shrinkage occurs during the drying process. A tight hold will also allow the heads to splay out. Elastic bands or twine are good, stem tape also works. An excellent, inexpensive medium is a strip cut from a pair of used stockings or tights. About 30 ties can be made from just one pair. Cut out circles from the leg then snip once to make a strip. Knot the strip tightly round the stems and use the ends to tie round your support. If you use twine or string, use a slipknot as this will automatically tighten as the stems dry and shrink. If the material is drying in an area where it can be seen tie ribbon or raffia round the string in a colour that co-ordinates with your decor.

5   If the correct conditions are met your flowers should dry quickly with good colour retention. A rose will take about seven days, smaller flowers a little less time, larger ones a little more. Most flowers will have dried within a couple of weeks. You will know that they are ready once they feel completely dry to the touch. You can break one of the stems to see if it snaps easily. If they have been dried in an unheated shed or garage, they should be removed before the damp weather sets in. Also remove from a site that has direct sunlight.

6   If you wish to use your flowers at a later date store them in boxes in a dry, airy place and add a little desiccant such as silica gel or Flower Dry to absorb any moisture that may enter the box (see Appendix 3). Make a few holes in the box to allow air circulation. Take care to store away from mice and moths – you could add a few mothballs to your box. The riper the grasses and wheat are when you dry them, the

more attractive they will be as food! If you are storing more than one box mark each box with the plant material it contains.

7   The dark will minimize the fading process. Alternatively, dried flowers always look good just hanging from where they have dried out but they will fade in time. The brighter the light, the quicker they will fade. Generally speaking dried flowers will keep good colour for up to a year.

Colours that remain truest seem to be those that are closest to the pure hue. Dark colours go even darker and light colours even paler. Dark red roses will go nearly black in colour. Pale yellow roses turn a dull cream.

Virtually all plant material that dries on the stem in the open can be dried upright in the home. Examples are dock, Chinese lanterns, poppy seedheads.

APPENDIX 2

Preserving with glycerine

Most people interested in preserved flowers will have seen bunches hanging up to dry. Not everyone will be aware that plant material, particularly foliage, can be preserved by adding glycerine to the water so that in time the plant material becomes flexible, water resistant and capable of lasting a lifetime. Many of the leaves particularly responsive to this form of preservation have a wonderful smooth texture which is a natural foil to the busier texture of many dried flowers.

Glycerine is a colourless sticky liquid that can be purchased from any chemist. Once mixed with hot water it can be taken up by the plant's stem. Some of the water is used by the plant and the remainder is lost in the atmosphere. The glycerine, however, because of its viscosity remains in the plant tissue and gives it permanent support. Antifreeze has many of the same properties as glycerine – it is a viscose solution that can be mixed with water. The results are not as consistent but the different coloured antifreezes can tint your glycerined material successfully.

If the procedure is followed correctly you will be able to retain the shape and form of many different types of foliage but the colour must change. There is no neat rule as to the colour it will turn but the vast majority of foliage will assume a shade or tint of brown. Box will turn to a mellow cream, rhododendron darkest brown and the rest somewhere in between. There are exceptions, for instance variegated eleagnus turns yellow, but they are rare. The colour can be changed by dyes. This is discussed below.

Few flowers can be preserved by the glycerine process because:

● It takes time for the plant structure to absorb glycerine and the flower-heads would wilt before the glycerine could reach them.
● The structure of flowers is too delicate for the absorption of a heavy liquid.

- The colour change, although fine in foliage, is rather restrictive when such glorious colour retention can be gained by other preserving methods.

Method

1 Prepare your stems for preserving. Evergreens can be preserved throughout the year but not when putting forth new growth in the spring as this new growth wilts too easily. Deciduous foliage that loses its leaves during the winter must be preserved at the height of its strength, i.e. not when the leaves are newly formed in the spring or in late summer when the stems are preparing to shed their leaves for the winter. Timing will be different according to the part of the country but generally late June or early July is ideal.

Remove any damaged leaves and those near the bottom of the stem. Cut the stem ends on the slant to allow the easy intake of liquid and place in water in a cool place for several hours so that the plant becomes 'turgid', i.e. fully charged with water. This will mean the plant material and particularly the outer and taller leaves will be less likely to wilt before the slower moving glycerine and water mixture arrives. Do not crush the stem ends. This only damages the stem and causes bacteria to multiply rapidly.

2 Take a jam jar and fill it about a quarter full with glycerine. Add to it double the amount of very hot water so that the jar is three-quarters full. Stir well so that the glycerine and water form a mixture. When purchasing glycerine buy the largest amount possible as it can be kept indefinitely and proves a better buy. If you wish to add colour to your plant material add a few drops of dye, in the colour mix of your choice. You may need to experiment a little to get the exact colour required.

3 Place the plant material to be preserved in the jam jar containing the mixture. It should rise approximately 8–10 cm (3–4 in) up the stem. If the stems are long place the jam jar in a bucket so that the stems can rest against the rim and thus avoid the risk of falling over. Heavy textured leaves can be wiped with glycerine before the stem ends are placed in the mixture. Ivy leaves and small sprays of leaves respond well to being totally submerged in the mixture.

4 Place the plant material in a dry area and monitor the progress of the glycerine mixture climbing up the stem and into the leaves. You will notice some degree of colour change as the mixture moves upwards.

5 The stems can be removed when the entire stem and leaves have

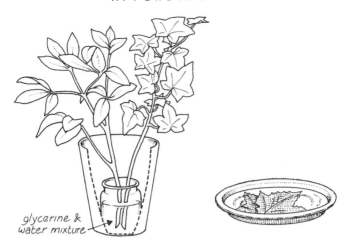

glycerine &
water mixture

received the mixture. Add more glycerine mixture, in the same proportions as step 2, if all is taken up by the stem before preservation is complete. Do not leave the foliage in the mixture once it has changed colour, especially if it is going to be left in a humid atmosphere, as the glycerine will ooze out. This can be particularly disastrous if dye has been used. If the leaves are slightly greasy wash them in a soapy water. Rinse, allow to dry on a piece of kitchen towel and, if not being displayed immediately, store this preserved material in a dry place.

6   The glycerine mixture can be reused again and again. Pass the used mixture through muslin or a fine sieve to remove any bits. If you find the mixture becomes mouldy, add a drop of bleach to minimise the risk of this recurring.

7   Do not store in plastic bags as this will cause the glycerined stems and leaves to sweat.

—— Tips to ensure success ——

1   Smooth leaves take the glycerine treatment better than those with a rough texture. Beech, box, escallonia, eleagnus and cotoneaster are good examples.

2   As a general rule, evergreens that grow slowly last well in water once cut. They also respond well to the glycerine treatment as they are

less likely to wilt before the process is complete. The process can, however, take quite a few weeks.

3 Perhaps the most sure-safe foliage to glycerine is beech. Green beech is, perhaps, easier than copper beech. The earlier it is treated in the season the darker it will go. The process is brief and you will consider yourself extremely clever when you view your first results.

4 Allow the preserving process to take place away from draughts. This will help to prevent the material drying out before the process is complete.

5 The best results seem to take place during the warmer summer months when the mixture is rapidly taken up by the foliage.

6 If the stems are long or the leaves large wipe each leaf with a cloth impregnated with the glycerine mixture from time to time.

7 Some plant material does retain a green tinge but if dye is not added the vast majority of plant material will change colour to tints, tones and shades of brown. If you place your material in direct sunlight it will be partly bleached, resulting in a much paler colour.

Preserving by glycerine and the hang drying technique

A combination of the two methods is ideal for:

1 Fragile, bushy flowering stems which would be too easily damaged by just hang drying and would lose their lightness of colour by preserving only with glycerine. Examples are *Alchemilla mollis* and gypsophila.

2 Plant material where the flowers or bracts are enhanced by the colour change. Bells of Ireland (*Molucella laevis*) turn a lovely cream colour when preserved by a combination of the two methods.

3 Plant material where the glycerine does not move sufficiently quickly up the stem for the preserved tip to take the mixture before wilting, such as Bells of Ireland.

Method

1 Place the stem ends in the glycerine mixture and after a few days hang the stems upside down to dry.

APPENDIX 3

Preserving with a desiccant

A desiccant is a substance that absorbs moisture. If flowers are covered by a form of desiccant and are left there for a short period of time – as a rough guide a few days to a few weeks – they will be preserved in their three dimensional shape for a considerable period of time, if kept under certain conditions.

The advantages of this method of preserving are that the shape and the colour are kept virtually the same as when fresh. The disadvantage is that a flower preserved by this means is brittle and therefore easily damaged unless protected under glass. To keep good colour the flowers will need to be kept out of strong sunlight.

Although sand, borax, allum and even soap powder can be used as a desiccant there are two mediums easily available that perform so well that only they will be mentioned in depth. Silica gel is the first. It can be purchased or ordered from chemists but the granules are usually so large that they need to be ground before use. Maureen Foster's preserving crystals, however, are ready to use and are excellent. Another product is Flower Dry. This is composed of small clay pellets which are amazingly pleasant to touch and use. Excellent instructions on how to use these products accompany each box. The mail order addresses for these two products are given at the back of this book.

Suitable plant material

1 Large single-petalled or deeply volumetric specimen flowers are ideal for preserving by this method, such as daffodils, lilies and iris.

2   Only treat perfect specimens, just prior to maturity.

3   Select plant material that is dry. If there is any moisture on the flower place it first in a vase with water until the head is dry.

4   Do include some leaves. They can be preserved at any stage of their growth and from just about any tree or shrub. Even the coloured autumnal leaves can be preserved by desiccant. Because they become brittle when preserved by this method it is a good idea to preserve about double the amount you think you will need.

Method

1   Cut off the stems to within approximately 2.5 cm (1 in) of the flower-head.

2   Add a false stem of wire. The methods are described in Appendix 5. As the flower dries it tightens on the wire.

3   The process can be speeded up by placing the flower on a little desiccant in a non-metallic container in a microwave. If you are using a microwave leave a short stem or pierce a hole in the plant material for wiring after drying. Timing will depend on the microwave you are using. If you understand your microwave and are interested in preserving by this means, do experiment. There is an excellent small book on preserving in the microwave by Titia Joosten which is mentioned on the recommended reading list at the back of this book.

4   Place the flower face up, with the stem twisted or coiled, on a bed of desiccant. Gently pour desiccant around the flower and then between the petals. Add desiccant until no part of the flower is showing. Do not crowd flowers together in the container – leave space between each one.

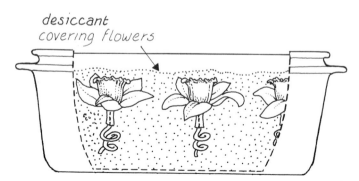

desiccant covering flowers

5   Leave the container open if left in a warm, very dry place. If there is any likelihood of damp air, add the lid and strap it down well.

6   Leave the tin or box in a warm, dry place, such as an airing cupboard for as long as necessary. Some flowers may only need 24 hours. For your first attempts keep checking every few days. If the flower is damp and soft instead of dry and papery, leave it in the desiccant.

7   To remove, pour off the desiccant in a steady stream with one hand below the container to catch the flower. You can use a sieve.

8   Until you wish to arrange your flowers you can stick the wire ends into a small piece of foam and put them in a box or tin with a little desiccant to trap any moisture in the atmosphere.

9   The flowers should be sprayed with an acrylic sealant to help them to last longer. This could be purchased in a craft shop. Maureen Foster's or Oasis's Super Surface Sealers are ideal for this purpose.

10 All desiccants need to be thoroughly dried out before re-using. Follow the instructions carefully. Most desiccants can be dried out by placing them in a low oven for about an of hour or by placing them in a microwave for about 10 minutes.

APPENDIX 4

Preserving by pressing

Pressing flowers is a gentle craft which can give hours of absorbing pleasure. You can create exquisite cards and gifts for minimal cost. Pressed flowers are used for many decorative purposes and there are many excellent books dealing solely with this means of plant preservation.

Flowers are pressed to fix their shape while the water content is removed. In an unpressed specimen, this would cause wilting. In this instance the word shape is used rather than form as the flower loses its three-dimensional form. Colourful leaves that are pressed in the autumn keep their colour – perhaps because dehydration is already under way.

To press flowers there is no need to go to the expense of buying a flower press, but if you have one, or especially wish to buy one, there should be instructions on how to use it. An old telephone directory presses flowers inexpensively and effectively. Some people use blotting paper, kitchen towelling or toilet tissue between the sheets of the directory to absorb the moisture given off by the flowers but as the paper that constitutes telephone directories is also absorbent there is no real need.

– Suitable plant material for pressing –

1 More delicate flowers, and in particular wild flowers, are easy to press and indeed often look better. Daisies, buttercups and celandines are exceptionally attractive when pressed but do pick daisies before the centre develops. Observe the Rules of the Countryside and only take from common plants where they grow in abundance. Never uproot any plant.

2   The flatter the flower-head the easier the flower will be to press. However, flowers that have a volumetric shape (think of lobelia, fuchsia or snowdrops) are also useful but they will need to be pressed on their sides. Fleshy flowers, leaves and stems contain a lot of water and are consequently more difficult to press efficiently.

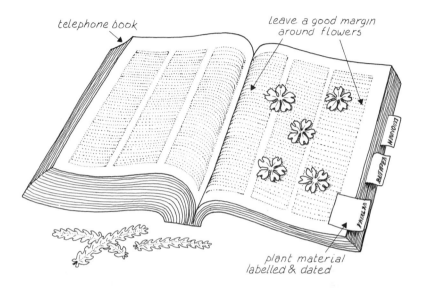

telephone book

leave a good margin around flowers

plant material labelled & dated

3   Colour changes occur during the pressing process. Yellows, pinks and greys retain their colour well. Most blue flowers dry well but some fade quite rapidly when exposed to strong light. Many white flowers turn cream or brown. Reds often turn beige.

4   Small plant material is generally more useful, particularly when you are starting out.

5   Small leaves are an essential part of any design. Tendrils and stems are also useful. Leaves with a toothed edging such as herb Robert and kerria, or those with intricate leaflets such as silver leaf are exquisite when pressed.

6   Large, plain oval or round leaves can look uninteresting and heavy when they lose the third dimension but they can be cut and shaped to create wonderful landscape pictures.

7   The flowers must be picked at the peak of their flowering and not after or they will be likely to fall apart during the pressing process.

8   Large three-dimensional flowers such as orchids, daffodils and garden roses can be pressed successfully but they are more difficult. The flowers often need to be taken to pieces, the individual parts pressed and then glued back together. So leave these until you are feeling confident and have successfully pressed smaller flatter flower heads such as pansies, dog roses, buttercups and daisies. Primulas press most effectively. The paler colours and yellow retain their colour exceptionally well.

9   Only press perfect specimens.

Method

1   Work from the back of the telephone directory and leave about 20 pages between each page of flowers. This gives sufficient density of paper to absorb the moisture and to even out any bumpiness of surface created by the flowers. Avoid placing plant material too close to the margin as when you turn the pages on top of them they do move slightly towards the edge.

2   Remove the stem from the flower and press the two parts separately. If the flowers are pressed over the stems there will be an unnatural line through the flowers.

3   Use a different page for each variety of flower or leaf or tendril as each has a different thickness and more delicate flowers may not be properly pressed. The pressure needs to be uniform.

4   Leave space between each flower and do not place flowers too close to the spine.

5   If the centre of the flower is hard, press it down firmly with a finger.

6   Stems may be Sellotaped into curves. Curves are often more useful in designs than straight lines.

7   Label the contents and date. Yellow Post-Its are ideal for this or you can allow a strip of paper to protrude from the book. You may think you would never forget the name of the leaf or flower, but you could be surprised.

8   Put heavier books or more telephone directories on top of the book of flowers. Store them in a dry, slightly warm atmosphere.

9   Plant material intended for flower pictures should be pressed for at least three weeks and if possible three to six months. The longer the flowers are left the more paper-thin the material will become. As a consequence the colours will not fade as rapidly when exposed to light, although colour intensity and lasting quality varies according

to the flowers. If you want to send a pressed flower card and you cannot wait longer than a few days give the dehydration process a start by placing the plant material between brown paper and pressing it with a warm iron.

10   If you wish to remove flowers that seem to have stuck to the pages, use a sharp knife, a nail file or a razor blade.

11   Larger pieces of foliage can be pressed between sheets of newspaper under the carpet. Suitable foliage could include oak, maple, beech, bracken and ferns. Do not leave it there for ever so that it still retains some flexibility.

12   If you need your book for further pressings allow the paper to completely dry out before re-use and store each variety of material in a paper bag, an envelope or a bag with a see-through front which you may be able to obtain from your local bakery. Alternatively, you can use a rigid file box and store the pressed flowers and foliage between blotting paper.

13   If you wish to improve on the colours of your pressed flowers, use a washable felt-tipped pen and use a finger to blend in the colour. Alternatively use poster paint diluted with water. Details on how to make your pressed plant materials into cards and pictures is explained in Chapter 15 on seasonal gifts and decorations.

The Pressed Flower Craft Guild is an organisation whose aims are to raise the general standard of the craft, to arrange teaching and seminar facilities where members can share expertise and experience, and to encourage work improvement through a series of optional assessments to gain bronze, silver or gold awards. If you are interested in the craft of pressed flowers do contact the membership secretary whose address is given in Appendix 6.

The National Association of Flower Arranging Societies (NAFAS) also has many talented members, who give talks and demonstrations on the craft of pressed flowers at clubs throughout the country. Addresses of local clubs can be obtained by direct contact with NAFAS. The address is also given in Appendix 6.

APPENDIX 5

Wiring

Wiring can give strength to weak stems, provide a stem where none existed and allow preserved material to be flexed over the rim of the container to give an effect of freer flow. A few stems can be held together with florists' tape but if you practise simple wiring you will find that this is easier than using florists' tape and more effective. When you have wired your stems you will need to cover the wires with stem tape.

Stem tape

Stem tape is used to cover the wires and to give them a natural appearance. It comes on a reel and is available in various colours – white, brown, black – but it is green that is probably the most useful. It is rather like a continuous thin strip of crepe paper. When stretched it adheres to the wire although it does not appear to be sticky unless it is kept in too hot an atmosphere. It needs a little practice to work well but it is worth the effort. For fine work it is often easier to split the stem tape in two.

Wires

Wires can be purchased in a bundle or on a reel. As a broad generalisation wire can be divided into:

- Stub wire
- Reel wire
- Rose wire
- Mossing pins (sometimes called German pins)

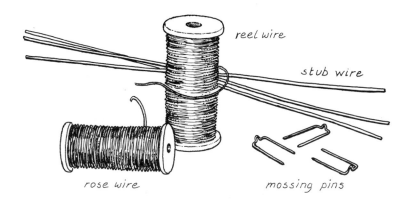

reel wire

stub wire

rose wire

mossing pins

Stub Wire

Stub wire is sold in different strengths. Trying to differentiate between the strengths can sometimes appear to necessitate the possession of a Masters Degree. To confuse us all they are sometimes marked with the metric figure and sometimes with the standard wire gauge figure. With metric figures the heavier the wire the higher the number, and with standard figures the heavier the wire the lower the figure. Most work can be covered with the acquisition of light wires (22 or 24 (0.7 or 0.56)) and medium wires, 20 (0.9). If you need heavy wires you can simply put two medium weight wires together, and bind them together with stem tape.

Stub wire can be purchased in different lengths. The longer ones (30 cms (12 in)) are usually the best buy as they can be cut down into shorter lengths. The price varies little. Stub wire that has not been treated with a green coating does rust so store it in a dry place. If you do buy several different weights store them upright in tall coffee jars.

Stub wires can be used for:

Creating false stems

Stub wires are used to give false stems to preserved plant material that has weak or broken stems. Flowers that have weak or brittle stems benefit from being wired. This also has the added attraction of making the stem flexible so that it can be angled in any direction. It is easier to wire flowers when they are fresh. Cut off all but the last 2.5 cm (1 in) of the natural stem.

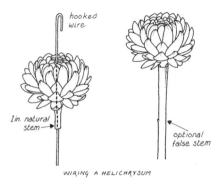

hooked
wire

1in. natural
stem

optional
false stem

WIRING A HELICHRYSUM

Push a medium gauge wire up the remaining stem and through the centre of the flowers. The wire corrodes a little and sticks to the flower. For extra security the wire can be pushed through the flower, a hook made and pulled back into the centre of the flower. If the helichrysums or other flowers are already dried simply glue the wire to the bottom of the flower. The wires can be slipped into a robust dried flower stem belonging to another flower, grass or seedhead.

Wiring cones and nuts

Cones

For small to medium-sized cones wrap a medium gauge wire round the lowest part of the cone between the scales, pulling it tight but leaving each end loose. Take the loose ends, bring them both together under the base of the cone and twist to form a stalk.

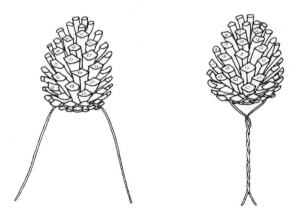

For larger cones use two wires. Hold both wires horizontally, one each side of the cone and force each one as low as possible between the scales. Twist the two ends at each side together. Pull under the base of the cone and twist together to form a stalk.

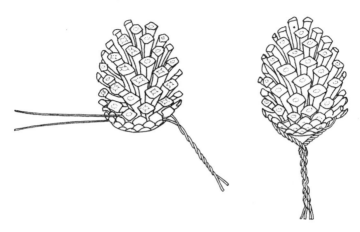

Nuts

Beech nuts usually have a short stalk which is just sufficient to poke into foam. If you need a longer stalk, take a wire and pass it over and down between the 'petals' and form a stalk by twisting one side of the wire round the other. Walnuts are easy to wire. Insert a strong wire or cocktail stick through the join on the base of the walnut and add a dab of glue to keep it securely in place. Brazil nuts and almonds are tough and need a drill to make a hole before a wire can be inserted. This is not the easiest of tasks! Chestnuts can be easily penetrated with a wire. Cover the wires with stem tape. For cones and nuts the brown stem tape appears the most natural.

Bunching plant material

In some dried flower designs the plant material is inserted into the foam in bunches to give stronger impact of colour, form or texture. Bunching is also used when you wish to bring more delicate plant material into scale with larger flowering varieties (see page 22). The method is very simple. Take a wire and bend it so that one 'leg' is longer than the other. Hold it against your bunch of stems so that the shorter wire protrudes beyond the end of the stems. Leaving a short loop at the top wind the longer 'leg' of wire around the stems and the other wire.

Choose the weight and length of wire according to the robustness of the material to be bunched.

Easier insertion of stems

Some dried flower arrangers wire every stem in order to make the insertion into the foam easier. Although it is not really necessary it is very useful to do this if your plant material is brittle, if the stems are not strong, or if your design is nearing completion and there is little room for manœuvrability. The method of wiring is the same as when bunching.

You can always stem tape brittle stems first to make them stronger before wiring.

Reel wire

Reel wire is used when you need a continuous length of wire as when binding spagnum moss on to a wire frame in order to create a floral ring or joining bunches together to form a garland. Reel wire is now available in colours such as red and blue and, if wrapped round moss balls, can become a design feature.

Rose wire

Rose wire can be purchased either on a reel or in bundles, usually 15 cm (6 in) long. If you want to be economical, buy a reel as it can always be cut into the shorter lengths. Rose wire is used for more delicate work. Small delicate bunches would be joined together with rose wire. It is also used to give a stalk to individual leaves and to make them flexible. There are two ways this can be done.

Method 1 (for strong leaves such as glycerined ivy or laurel)

Make a neat stitch through the back of the leaf, about two thirds of the way up. Place a finger firmly on the stitch as you draw the two wire ends downwards so that they are parallel with each other and the remaining end of stalk. Wrap the longer end of wire around the other wire and the stem.

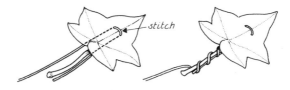

Cover the wire with stem tape and cut to the length required. A neat piece of Sellotape can be placed over the back of the stitch to minimise tearing.

Method 2 (for more delicate leaves such as glycerined beech)

For more delicate leaves a fine wire can simply be bent into a hairpin. The top of the loop is placed against the bottom half of the leaf. The longer 'leg' of the wire is then wrapped round the other and the remaining end of stalk leaving the loop free.

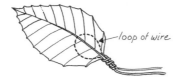

Cover the wire with stem tape and cut to the length required. If you wish to give more strength to the stem you can add a length of stub wire before binding the stem with stem tape.

Mossing pins

These are sometimes called German pins. They come in various lengths and look very similar to hair pins. For dried flower work shorter pins are generally more useful. They are wonderful for securing moss to floral foam. If you cannot find these simply take a medium wire, cut into 8–10 cm (3–4 in) lengths, bend and use as required.

——— APPENDIX 6 ———

——— Additional plant material ———

All plant material can be dried, and this appendix lists but a few. It includes the plants that have been used in the colour photographs that have not been mentioned in Appendix 4. The other plant material mentioned are either those varieties that dry well with good colour retention and are particularly effective in dried flower arrangements, or are easy to grow, or both qualities. Do make your own experiments with what you have available and add to this list which is, of course, not exhaustive.

Branching material

Acacia (Mimosa)

Although mimosa can be grown outside in some sheltered parts of the United Kingdom it is more usual to buy fresh mimosa from the florists. There are two types of mimosa commonly available, one has fern-like leaves and the other long lancelate leaves (as used in Figure 23 in the colour section). Both bear yellow button-like fluffy flowers. Mimosa hang dries extremely successfully with good colour retention. Do check that the flowers are not shedding pollen when purchasing.

Alchemilla mollis (Lady's mantle)

This is a delicate plant material that will give a lightness and softness to any design. The small, yellow-green flowers densely cover the numerous branches. It can be easily grown in the garden. One plant, if allowed to seed, will quickly spread and provide material for cutting twice a year during the summer months. It can be hang dried or left in glycerine for a few days before hanging, so that it becomes less brittle. It may be purchased fresh from most florists during the summer. Because each stem has numerous delicate branches they can get entangled, and the tips broken, so check this when buying alchemilla ready dried.

Eryngium maritimum (Sea holly)

Eryngium grows wild by the sea. It can also be easily grown in the garden or in a tub on the patio. It has branching sprays of small blue thistle-like flowers and has prickles on the stems. It is available fresh from many florists. It is sometimes dyed a deeper blue before being sold as dried plant material. This does not deter from its natural beauty. It can be dried by hanging or can simply be left in a vase.

Gypsophila paniculata (Baby's breath)

Gypsophila can give a lightness and interest to designs if used with discrimination. Although gypsophila can be grown in the garden the variety Bristol Fairy is available from florists most of the year and has large, double flowers excellent for drying. If buying ready dried check that the stems are not tangled and that the colour is an interesting creamy-white, rather than creamy-yellow – a colour which tends to develop with age.

Lunaria annua (Honesty)

Although honesty is a biennial it is rare that another purchase will ever have to be made as it self-seeds profusely. Pick honesty as soon as the pretty white or purple flowers have fallen and you will have wonderful green seedpods, perhaps with a tinge of deep purple-pink, that look enchanting in traditional flower baskets. Later in the year the silvery pods glisten in dried flower arrangements and, if placed when fresh in a little glycerine to which a drop of red dye has been added, the preserved honesty will be an interesting tint of pale pink. You can remove the two outer discs, to leave the inner central disc to create a more translucent effect. If purchasing dried, check that the pods or discs have not been damaged.

Solidago (Golden rod)

Solidago is considered a weed in some parts of the world. It grows very easily in this country and spreads rapidly. If picked just after the majority of the yellow flowers have come into bloom it will retain its freshness. Solidage can be purchased from florists, but only buy for drying if the flowers are coming into their peak of perfection. When buying dried, ensure that the colour is still interesting and the flowers are not dropping.

Line material

Chenopodium botrys (Ambrosinia)

The stems of ambrosinia hold many short, delicate, flowering branches of a clear green colour. It can be effectively used as line or branching plant material. It has the added bonus of having a fresh smelling fragrance. The seed can be sown directly into the soil in late spring. Alternatively, it can be purchased fresh from some florists. When purchasing dried, check that the tips of the spike have not drooped.

Liatris spicata (Blazing star)

The tall majestic spikes of liatris give a powerful presence to dried flower arrangements. The colour is strong and keeps well. The flowers develop from the top downwards and should be picked before the top flowers have opened too far. They have a strong stem and can be dried by hanging or by placing upright in a container. If they are placed in water any of the small leaves that cover the lower stem will go brown. When purchasing ready dried check that the flowering part of the stem has not been accidentally broken to show a white central core.

Mentha (Mint)

The mint family produce flowers in whorls round the stem. Mint has closely packed whorls of blue-pink flowers that give the impression of being spikes. Penny Royal, its close relation, has flowers in larger whorls, at wider intervals, down the stem. The colouring of both is soft and subtle and the fragrance sublime. Mint is so easy to grow and flowers well if it is not cut prior to flowering; although you may need to spray it for whitefly. It is now available dried from larger dried flower outlets.

Rumex (Dock or Sorrel)

Dock or sorrel (they are such close relations that they are classified together in this book) grows profusely in the wild and will dry simply placed upright in a container, if it has not already dried on the stem. It can be picked early in the season when green, or later when it has turned red-brown or even later in its development when it has turned brown. It is useful in all these stages of development.

Focal Flowers

Acroclinium

Acroclinium, like helichrysum, is termed an everlasting. It is found in a range of pinks, white and red, with either a yellow or black centre. They can be found in most dried flower outlets. Acroclinium can look very pretty but the papery flowers are easily damaged and can look rather sad if not well cared for, so check for this when purchasing.

Anaphalis margaritacea (Pearl everlasting)

This is a soft cream-white flower, clustered together in balls on rather a soft stem. It looks effective bunched and wired and can bring freshness and life to a design. If buying ready dried, check that the flowers are a clean cream-white colour and they are not over developed.

Gomphrena globosa (Globe amaranth)

Globe amaranth is an important component of many pot pourris for it is light, inexpensive, easily absorbs fragrant oils and dyes and retains its colour brilliantly. It has white, pink, purple or a strawberry red flower which look most attractive in dried flower designs, but the stems tend to be rather weak.

Helianthus annuus (Sunflower)

Sunflowers are easily grown in any sunny spot in the garden, on the patio and even in window boxes. If you have the space grow a variety of sizes. They dry extremely well and retain good colour. Try wiring the heads and drying the stems separately so that they can be added over the wires at a later stage. Sunflowers have been used in the decorated basket in Figure 14 in the colour section and in the cover photograph.

Lonas inodora

Lonas is like a small version of *Achillea filipendulina*. It has a small, flat golden head and is particularly useful in small designs which would be overpowered by the large heads of achillea. It is an annual and has a good strong stem, with excellent colour retention. It can be dried by hanging or by placing upright in a container. Most dried flower suppliers stock lonas.

Tagetes (Marigold)

Yellow and orange marigolds give bright pure colour which is largely retained when dried. The large double marigolds can be easily grown in the garden and picked just before they are fully open. As the colour is strong and hot use them carefully in a well planned colour scheme. Orange marigolds have been used in Figure 15 in the colour section.

Physalis franchetii (Chinese lanterns)

One small plant of physalis will spread and produce vibrant orange calyces, encasing the fruit, every year. It can be planted in shade and in poor soil and still it will keep producing fruit. The bracts are a pure orange and as such are wonderful in autumnal displays but can be more difficult to use at different times of the year, as it tends to overpower much dried plant material. They can be hung up to dry but if you feel that the bracts are drying at an awkward angle to the main stem you can continue the drying in a vase. Dried physalis are expensive as their hollow shape makes them susceptible to damage.

Sedum spectabile

Sedums are an easy perennial which grow year after year, without problems. The variety 'Autumn Joy' produces flat heads which are a mass of sultry pink flowers. The stems should be picked when firm and the flowers have been given a little time to develop, but be sure to pick them before they turn brown. Sedum is often sold at bazaars and fêtes in the autumn.

Rodanthe

Rodanthe is similar in appearance to *Acroclinium*. It has papery round flowers, usually seen in the natural pink or white or dyed to various shades. If buying fresh the flower should be still closed. Check when buying dried that their fresh appeal has not been spoiled by careless handling for they are easily damaged.

Scabiosa caucasica (Scabious)

Scabious is a hardy perennial that freely gives blue or white flowers during the summer months. The spherical seedheads that follow are lovely in flower designs but are extremely delicate and consequently are easily damaged. Scabious tends to be expensive to buy but can be easily dried in the home.

Xeranthemum annuum

Xeranthemum is another everlasting flower with straw-like petals. It is easy to grow and easy to dry, and is widely available from dried flower stockists. You will notice on unwrapping Xeranthemum that there is a long length of stem in proportion to the flowering head, so if you are using this flower in a medium or large design it is advisable to bunch them. If buying fresh the flowers should be closed because an open centre often turns grey during the drying process. When purchasing ready dried, ensure that the usual white or violet colouring is clear and not been damaged by rain.

APPENDIX 7

Useful Addresses and recommended reading

Please send a large s.a.e. with all enquiries.

Courses

Day courses on all aspects of
flower and garden design:
Judith Blacklock School of
Flower Design
52 Suffolk Road
London SW13 9NR

Publications

The Flower Arranger Magazine
Available through Flower Clubs
affiliated to NAFAS or direct
from:
Taylor Bloxham Ltd
Nugent Street
Leicester
LE3 5HH

Flora International Magazine
Available from newsagents or
direct from:

Fishing Lodge Studio
77 Bulbridge Road
Wilton
Salisbury
Wilts SP2 0LE
Tel: 0722 743207

Desiccants

Flower Dry
Moira Clinch
The Greenhouse Studio
10 The Green
Mountsorrel
Leics LE12 7AF
Tel: 0533 375046

Maureen Foster's Flower
Preserving Crystals
77 Bulbridge Road
Wilton
Salisbury
Wilts SP23 0LE

Glycerine

Flowercraft
18 High Street
Chapel-en-le-Frith
Stockport
Cheshire SK12 6HD
Telefax: 0298 812491

Associations

NAFAS (National Association of
Flower Arranging Societies)
21 Denbigh Street
London SW1V 2HF
Tel: 071 828 5145

The Pressed Flower Guild
Membership Secretary
   Mrs Lloyd
92 Langley Walk
Langley Green
Crawley
West Sussex RH11 7LR

Specialist shops and mail order companies

Other addresses can be found in
issues of *The Flower Arranger*
and *Flora International*
magazines.

G Baldwin & Co
171–173 Walworth Road
London SE17 1RW
Tel: 071 703 5550
(Shop and excellent mail order
list for all items for pot pourri)

The Flower Cellar
161 Wilton Road
Salisbury
Wilts SP2 7JQ
Tel: 0722 333433
Shop and mail order service

The Floral Workshop
Hamptons Cottage
Oxenhoath Road
Hadlow
Nr Tonbridge
Kent TN11 9SS
Tel: 0732 810223
Shop only

Moira Clinch
The Greenhouse Studio
10 The Green
Mountsorrel
Leics LE12 7AF
Tel: 0533 375046
Shop and mail order service

Kay Gunner
Old Portsmouth Road
Thursley
Godalming
Surrey GU8 6NJ
Tel: 0252 702076
Christmas and floral crafts

Focal Flowers
17 Cross Flatts Avenue
Beeston
Leeds LS11 7BE
Tel: 0532 774001
Mail order service

Secretts
Hurst Farm
Chapel Lane
Milford
Godalming
Surrey GU8 5HU
Tel: 0483 427971
Shop only

The Diddy Box
132–134 Belmont Road
Astley Bridge
Bolton
Lancs BL1 7AN
Tel: 0204 592405
Shop and mail order service
(please enclose £1.00 to cover
cost of catalogue)

Western Wire Ltd
Forest Vale Industrial Estate
Cinderford
Glos GL14 2PH
Tel: 0594 824222
Wires of all descriptions supplied
by mail order

Impress
Slough Farm
Westhall
Halesworth
Suffolk IP19 8RN
Tel: 0986 781422

Mail order for blank cards and
other stationery for pressed
flower work including self-
adhesive film.

Specialist Crafts (Dryad) Ltd
PO Box 247
Leicester LE1 9QS
Tel: 0533 510405
Mail order and shop selling
everything for specialist crafts –
adhesives, transparent self-
adhesive film, flower presses,
etc. Excellent catalogue for a
nominal amount, reimbursed on
placement of minimum order.

Simply Garlands
51 Albion Road
Pitstone
Bucks LU7 9AY
Tel: 0296 661425

Flower Dyes

Carters of Blackburn
29 Carham Road
Blackburn
Lancs BB1 8NX
Telefax: 0254 675025

Recommended reading

Joosten, Titia; *Flower Drying with a Microwave, Techniques and Projects*.
    Sterling Lark, 1985
Sheen, Joanna and Caroline Alexander; *Dried Flower Gardening*. Ward
    Lock, 1991
Conder, Susan; *Dried Flowers*. Marshall Cavendish, 1988

Scott, Margaret Kennedy; *Pressed Flowers and Flower Pictures.*
Batsford, 1988

Bussi, Cathy; *Pressed Flowers, A Creative Guide.* New Holland, 1988

Foster, Maureen; *Flower Preserving for Beginners.* Pelham Books

—— *The Art of Preserved Flower Arrangements.* Pelham Books

—— *Creating Pictures with Preserved Flowers.* Pelham Books

—— *The Flower Arranger's Encyclopedia of Preserving and Drying.*
Pelham Books, 1991

Coleman, Rona and Sylvia Pepper; *The Encyclopedia of Flower Arranging.* New Burlington Books, 1988

Mierhof, Annette and Marijke den Boer-Vlamings; *The Dried Flower
Book.* Herbert Press, 1981

Hillier, Malcolm and Colin Hilton; *The Complete Book of Dried Flowers.*
Dorling Kindersley, 1986

Black, Penny; *The Book of Pot Pourri.* Dorling Kindersley, 1989

Specialist seed companies

Chiltern Seeds
Bortree Style
Ulverston
Cumbria LA12 7PB
Tel: 0229 581137
Chiltern Seeds has a readable and informative brochure which stocks
nearly all the dried flower seed mentioned in this book.

John Chambers' Wild Flower Seeds
15 Westleigh Road
Barton Seagrave
Kettering
Northants
NN15 5AJ
Tel: 0933 652562
John Chambers has a large range of both wild and cultivated grass
species, herbs, everlasting flowers and wild flowers which have interesting seedheads.

INDEX